Coins to Fortune

Launching Your Vending Machine Venture: From Initial Investment to Strategic Placement, Decoding the Blueprint and Maximizing Profits

Richard Feldstone

The information contained in this book is intended for educational purposes only and is not intended to replace the advice of a professional. The author and publisher have made every effort to ensure the accuracy of the information herein. However, the author and publisher make no representation or warranties with respect to the accuracy or completeness of the contents of this book and specifically disclaim any implied warranties of merchantability or fitness for a particular purpose. The information contained herein is provided on an "as is" basis without warranty of any kind.

The author and publisher shall have no liability or responsibility to any person or entity with respect to any loss or damage caused, or alleged to be caused, directly or indirectly by the information contained in this book.

Trademarks, service marks, and logos appearing in this book are the property of their respective owners. They are used for identification purposes only and not for endorsement, sponsorship, or affiliation.

Summary

Chapter 1: Setting the Stage for Success

In life, success is something that we all strive for. Whether it is in our personal relationships, our careers, or our overall well-being, the desire to achieve success burns within each of us. But what is it that separates those who reach great heights from those who fall short? The answer lies in our ability to set the stage for success.

In this chapter, we will explore the key elements that contribute to creating the foundation for a successful life. From mindset and goal setting to self-discipline and resilience, we will delve deep into the intricacies of paving the way towards our desired outcomes. So, let us embark on this journey together, as we unravel the secrets to setting the stage for success.

Mindset: The Key to Unleashing Potential

At the very core of setting the stage for success lies the power of mindset. Our thoughts, beliefs, and attitudes shape our reality, and it is through cultivating a growth-oriented mindset that we can unlock our true potential. The way we perceive ourselves and the world around us plays a crucial role in determining our trajectory towards success.

When we adopt a fixed mindset, our focus is on maintaining the status quo. We see our abilities, intelligence, and talents as fixed traits, minimizing the possibility for growth and improvement. On the other hand, a growth mindset emphasizes the belief that our abilities can be developed through dedication and hard work. Embracing this perspective allows us to see challenges as opportunities for growth rather than setbacks.

Goal Setting: Navigating the Path to Success

Once we have established the right mindset, the next step towards setting the stage for success is goal setting. Without clear objectives, we wander aimlessly, lacking a sense of direction. Setting meaningful goals not only gives us a target to strive for but also provides a roadmap to guide us along the journey.

When setting goals, it is important to ensure they are specific, measurable, attainable, relevant, and time-bound, commonly known as SMART goals. Specific goals focus our attention and energy, measurable goals allow us to track our progress, attainable goals keep us motivated, relevant goals align with our values, and time-bound goals create a sense of urgency.

However, it is not enough to simply establish goals; we must also cultivate a strong sense of purpose and vision to bring them to life. When our goals align with our passions and values, they become fuel for our motivation, propelling us forward in the face of adversity.

Self-Discipline: The Bridge between Goals and Achievement

While setting goals is crucial, it is self-discipline that acts as the bridge between mere aspirations and actual accomplishment. Self-discipline involves the ability to resist immediate gratification in favor of long-term rewards. It is a key trait that propels successful individuals towards their desired outcomes, even when faced with temptations and distractions.

To cultivate self-discipline, one must first identify and understand their personal triggers that lead to complacency or indulgence. By recognizing these triggers, we gain the power to redirect our focus towards activities that align with our goals. Creating daily habits and routines that support our objectives can also be a powerful tool in reinforcing self-discipline.

Moreover, building resilience is an integral part of maintaining self-discipline. The path to success is rarely linear, and setbacks and failures are inevitable. Resilience allows us to bounce back from these challenges and stay committed to our goals. By reframing failure as a stepping stone to growth rather than a roadblock, we enhance our ability to maintain self-discipline in the face of adversity.

Creating a Supportive Environment

While intrinsic motivation and self-discipline are crucial in setting the stage for success, surrounding ourselves with a supportive environment can significantly enhance our journey. The people we associate ourselves with, the environments we immerse ourselves in, and the resources at our disposal all play a role in shaping our outcomes.

First and foremost, it is essential to build a network of individuals who share similar values and goals. Like-minded individuals can provide support, guidance, and accountability. Collaborating with others who are also on a path towards success can fuel our motivation and offer valuable insights.

Moreover, creating an environment conducive to growth is imperative. This can include cultivating a positive and inspiring physical space, whether that be a dedicated workspace or a clutter-free living area. Additionally, exposing ourselves to diverse perspectives through reading, attending seminars, or joining communities can expand our knowledge and challenge our beliefs, fostering personal growth.

In this chapter, we have explored the fundamental elements of setting the stage for success. A growth-oriented mindset, accompanied by clear and purposeful goal setting, provides the foundation for unleashing our potential. Yet, it is self-discipline that acts as the bridge between goals and achievement. Finally, creating a supportive environment, both in terms of people and physical spaces, enhances our journey towards success.

As we conclude this chapter, it is essential to acknowledge that setting the stage for success is an ongoing process rather than a destination. Life is a continuous journey of growth and learning, and our ability to adapt and remain flexible is paramount. In the following chapters, we will delve deeper into specific areas of personal and professional development to further guide you towards success, helping you actualize your aspirations and turn them into reality.

Understanding the Vending Landscape

Vending machines have become an integral part of our modern society. Whether we encounter them in offices, schools, hospitals, or public spaces, these automated devices offer convenience and ease in accessing a variety of goods and services. From snacks and beverages to electronics and hygiene products, vending machines cater to the needs and preferences of consumers on the go. In this chapter, we delve into the fascinating world of vending, exploring its rich history, evolving technologies, and the various factors that shape the vending landscape.

A Historical Perspective:

The concept of vending machines has roots dating back to ancient civilizations. The first documented example of an automated device can be traced back to ancient Egypt, where a holy water dispenser operated using coins. In more recent history, the concept experienced a resurgence during the Industrial Revolution in the 18th century. The invention of coin-operated devices, such as the first commercial vending machine developed by Richard Carlisle in 1822, laid the foundation for the vending industry as we know it today.

However, it wasn't until the 20th century that vending machines truly gained popularity. In the United States, post-war economic growth and advancements in technology fueled the rapid expansion of the vending industry. Companies like Coca-Cola and PepsiCo pioneered the introduction of automated vending machines for soft drinks, capitalizing on the convenience and accessibility they offered. This period marked the beginning of a significant shift in consumer behavior and the gradual integration of vending machines into various aspects of everyday life.

Types of Vending Machines:

The vending landscape has expanded significantly over the years, with a wide range of machines designed to cater to specific consumer needs. Today, we can categorize vending machines into several broad categories:

1. Snack and Beverage Machines: These machines are the most common and widely recognized in the vending industry. They offer a variety of snacks, sodas, and other beverages, providing a quick and convenient way for consumers to satisfy their cravings on the go. Snack and beverage machines have evolved to offer healthier options, reflecting the growing demand for more nutritious choices.

2. Hot Beverage Machines: From coffee and tea to hot chocolate and specialty beverages, hot beverage vending machines have gained popularity in recent years. With improved technology and the ability to customize drink preferences, these machines have found their

place in offices, gas stations, and other locations where people seek a hot drink to warm up or boost their energy levels.

3. Fresh Food Machines: Responding to the increasing demand for healthier meal options, fresh food vending machines have emerged as a convenient alternative to traditional fast food. These machines offer sandwiches, salads, fruit bowls, and other nutritious choices, leveraging refrigeration and advanced technology to maintain freshness and quality.

4. Retail and Electronics Machines: Vending machines are no longer limited to just food and beverages. Today, they can also dispense a wide range of items, including electronics, phone accessories, cosmetics, and even clothing. These machines provide customers with quick access to products they may need while on the go, eliminating the need for physical stores or long queues.

Technology Advancements:

As technology continues to advance, so too does the vending industry. The integration of cutting-edge technologies has revolutionized the user experience, making vending machines more efficient, versatile, and interactive. Here are some significant technological advancements in the vending landscape:

1. Cashless Payment Systems: Gone are the days when vending machines only accepted coins or paper currency. With the advent of

cashless payment systems, consumers can now use credit cards, mobile payment apps, and contactless methods to make purchases from vending machines. This has enhanced convenience and accessibility while reducing the risk of theft and vandalism.

2. Touchscreen Interfaces: Traditional push-button interfaces have given way to intuitive touchscreen displays, allowing for a more interactive and user-friendly experience. Touchscreens enable dynamic product displays, nutritional information, and customizable options, ensuring consumers can easily navigate through the available choices and make informed decisions.

3. Smart Vending: The rise of the Internet of Things (IoT) has paved the way for smart vending machines. These machines are equipped with sensors and connected to the internet, enabling real-time inventory monitoring, remote management, and data analytics. Smart vending optimizes operational efficiency, reduces downtime, and provides valuable insights into consumer preferences and buying patterns.

4. Product Customization: Vending machines now offer a higher degree of customization to meet diverse consumer preferences. From selecting the strength and flavor of a coffee to tailoring snack combinations or adjusting portion sizes, these machines allow consumers to personalize their purchases, creating a more personalized and satisfying experience.

Market Trends and Influencing Factors:

Several factors shape the vending landscape today, reflecting the changing needs and desires of consumers, as well as broader societal trends. Understanding these factors is crucial for vending operators and businesses looking to thrive in this competitive market. Let us explore some of the key market trends and influences:

1. Health and Wellness: As people become more health-conscious, the demand for healthier vending options has risen significantly. Vending operators have responded by offering a broader range of nutritious snacks, organic products, and fresh food choices. Partnering with local farms and suppliers has become common practice, ensuring access to high-quality and sustainable ingredients.

2. Sustainability and Eco-friendliness: With the increasing global focus on environmental preservation, vending operators are adopting sustainable practices in their operations. This includes using energy-efficient machines, incorporating recyclable packaging, and sourcing products from eco-friendly manufacturers. Furthermore, the concept of reverse vending machines, which reward users for recycling their bottles and cans, is gaining traction, demonstrating the industry's commitment to sustainability.

3. Contactless and Hygiene: The COVID-19 pandemic has reinforced the need for contactless transactions and enhanced hygiene measures. Vending operators are implementing touchless interfaces,

cashless payment options, and stringent sanitization protocols to reassure consumers of their safety. The pandemic has also highlighted the importance of adapting quickly to changes in consumer behavior, such as increased demand for personal hygiene products and disinfectants.

4. Localization and Personalization: In a world increasingly focused on individual preferences, vending operators are prioritizing localization and personalization. By stocking region-specific snacks, beverages, and products, vending machines can better meet the unique preferences of consumers in different locations. Additionally, utilizing data analytics and consumer insights allows operators to tailor product offerings and promotions based on specific demographics, leading to increased customer satisfaction and loyalty.

Understanding the vending landscape is essential for both consumers and businesses alike. From its humble beginnings to the integration of advanced technologies, vending machines have become an integral part of our daily lives. The industry continues to evolve, adapting to changing consumer demands, technological advancements, and societal trends. As we navigate this vending landscape, it is crucial to remain mindful of the fascinating history, emerging technologies, and key influencing factors that shape the future of this ubiquitous convenience.

Exploring the Potential of Vending Machines

Vending machines have come a long way since their humble beginnings. Once perceived as simple dispensers of snacks and soft drinks, they have evolved into sophisticated machines capable of dispensing a wide array of goods and services. This chapter aims to explore the untapped potential of vending machines, focusing on how they have revolutionized the consumer experience across various industries.

1. Enhanced Consumer Convenience:

Vending machines have become synonymous with convenience, providing consumers with access to products around the clock, in diverse locations. With advancements in technology, they have become more user-friendly, allowing individuals to effortlessly purchase everything from snacks and beverages to toiletries and electronics.

Moreover, the integration of touch screens, interactive displays, and customized interfaces have further simplified the purchasing process. These machines are designed to offer multiple payment options, including credit cards, mobile payments, and even cryptocurrencies, catering to a wider consumer base. Vending machines have transformed from merely being transactional to becoming interactive, engaging, and intuitive.

2. Diversifying Product Offerings:

One of the most significant advancements in vending machine technology is the increasing breadth of products that can be dispensed. Traditionally associated with snacks and soft drinks, these machines now cater to a wide range of needs. Today, one can find machines that dispense hot meals, gourmet coffee, fresh fruit, personal care items, and even prescription medications.

This diversification has created new opportunities for businesses to reach consumers in unique and unexpected locations. Popularized concepts, such as farmer's market vending machines and fully automated cafes, have made life more convenient for consumers, while offering new revenue streams for businesses.

3. Revolutionizing Retail:

The retail industry has witnessed a profound transformation with the integration of vending machines. These machines have not only disrupted traditional brick-and-mortar shops but have also elevated the consumer experience. Vending machines can act as miniature stores, making retail accessible beyond traditional business hours. They have proven to be particularly successful in niche industries, providing consumers with easy access to specialized products. For instance, vending machines that distribute cosmetics, electronics, or high-end jewelry present an opportunity for luxury brands to expand their reach.

4. Expanding Pathways for Food and Beverage Businesses:

Vending machines have changed the food and beverage landscape, offering alternative distribution channels for traditional restaurants and cafes. In high traffic areas like airports, train stations, and office complexes, vending machines allow food vendors to maximize their audience reach while reducing operational costs.

Moreover, advancements in vending machine technology have facilitated the availability of fresh and healthy options. By partnering with local producers and distributors, vending machines play a vital role in supporting community-based initiatives and healthy eating habits.

5. Improving Accessibility to Daily Essentials:

One of the most striking aspects of the evolution of vending machines is their ability to provide essential goods in underserved areas, often referred to as "vending deserts." These regions, lacking traditional retail infrastructure, benefit from vending machines that dispense basic essentials such as hygiene products, snacks, over-the-counter medications, and even fresh produce.

By empowering local entrepreneurs to set up small vending businesses, communities can gain access to affordable supplies without having to travel long distances. Vending machines ultimately bridge the gap in accessibility and create employment opportunities in underserved areas.

6. Deploying Smart Vending Machines:

The advent of artificial intelligence (AI) and the Internet of Things (IoT) has led to the emergence of smart vending machines. These machines employ algorithms that analyze purchasing patterns and adapt to consumer preferences in real-time. Furthermore, they enable remote monitoring of inventory, machine performance, and even temperature control to ensure product freshness.

Smart vending machines interact with consumers through voice recognition and facial recognition technology, deepening their engagement. This not only enhances the consumer experience but also provides valuable data and insights to businesses for better inventory management and targeted marketing initiatives.

7. Revolutionizing Autonomous Retail:

In recent years, the concept of cashier-less stores has gained popularity, largely influenced by innovative vending machine technology. Amazon Go stores and similar ventures utilize a combination of machine vision, sensor fusion, and advanced AI algorithms to enable consumers to enter, select products, and leave without any manual checkout process.

This pioneering approach has the potential to reshape the retail landscape by fundamentally altering the shopping experience. The integration of vending machine technology has made this autonomous retail model a reality, further reducing the need for human intervention.

In Vending machines have evolved far beyond their original purpose, becoming a catalyst for innovation and transforming the consumer experience across various industries. With their enhanced convenience, diversified product offerings, and integration of advanced technology, these machines have unleashed a whole new world of possibilities.

As consumer demands continue to evolve, vending machines will undoubtedly adapt to cater to emerging needs. By staying at the forefront of technology and embracing innovative business models, the potential of vending machines will only continue to grow, forever changing the way we access goods and services.

The Allure of Passive Income

In today's fast-paced and hectic world, many individuals find themselves yearning for financial freedom and the ability to live life on their own terms. The allure of passive income has captivated the minds of ambitious individuals looking to escape the shackles of the traditional 9-to-5 job. But what exactly is passive income, and why does it hold such a powerful appeal? In this chapter, we will delve deep into the concept of passive income, explore its advantages and disadvantages, and discover the various ways one can generate it. So sit back, relax, and prepare to explore the world of passive income.

Defining Passive Income:

To understand the attraction of passive income, we must first grasp its essence. In its simplest form, passive income is money earned with minimal effort or involvement on the earner's part after the initial investment of time, money, or resources. Unlike traditional forms of income, such as active employment or self-employment, passive income continues to flow even when you're not actively working. This alluring characteristic has led many to see passive income as the key to unlocking financial independence and financial abundance.

The Advantages of Passive Income:

One of the most significant advantages of passive income is its ability to provide individuals with a greater sense of freedom and flexibility. With passive income streams in place, one can have more control over their time, allowing them to pursue their passions, spend quality time with loved ones, or even explore new hobbies and ventures without the constant worry of financial stability. Passive income acts as a safety net, providing a stable foundation for individuals to build upon and explore new opportunities.

Furthermore, passive income possesses the potential for exponential growth. Unlike linear income, which is directly proportional to the time and effort invested, passive income can grow independently, accumulating and multiplying over time. This compounding effect allows individuals to achieve financial goals much quicker, as the income generated can be reinvested to create even more passive income. The high potential for growth is undoubtedly one of the most attractive aspects of passive income.

Generating Passive Income:

Now that we understand the allure of passive income let us explore the various avenues through which it can be generated. There are countless strategies and methods available; some require financial investment, others demand time and effort, while some may even blend both. Here are a few popular ways individuals generate passive income:

1. Rental Properties: Investing in real estate is a common method for generating passive income. By purchasing properties and renting them out, individuals can earn a consistent monthly income. While this method requires initial investment and proper property management, it can yield lucrative returns over time.

2. Dividend Stocks: Investing in dividend-paying stocks allows individuals to earn regular passive income through the distribution of company profits. By carefully selecting dividend stocks, investors can enjoy a steady stream of income without actively trading in the stock market.

3. Peer-to-Peer Lending: Peer-to-peer lending platforms have gained popularity in recent years as an alternative investment vehicle. Through these platforms, individuals can lend their money to borrowers, earning interest on the funds lent. This form of passive income can be relatively hands-off, but comes with a certain level of risk.

4. Online Businesses: The digital era has opened up numerous opportunities for creating passive income through online businesses. Whether it's creating and selling digital products, running an e-commerce store, or monetizing a blog or YouTube channel, the internet provides a wealth of possibilities for generating passive income.

5. Royalties and Intellectual Property: If you possess a creative streak, royalties and intellectual property can be excellent sources of passive income. Licensing music, patents, books, photographs, or any other intellectual property can generate recurring income for years

to come.

The Disadvantages of Passive Income:

While the prospect of passive income may seem enticing, it is crucial to consider its potential downsides. Passive income often requires an upfront investment of time, money, or both. Additionally, generating passive income often demands research, planning, and ongoing management to ensure success. For those seeking instant gratification, passive income may not provide immediate results, as it requires patience and a long-term commitment.

Moreover, certain passive income streams can come with risks. Market volatility, changes in regulations, and economic downturns can affect investments and other passive income sources. It is important to conduct thorough due diligence and diversify your income streams to mitigate these risks.

The allure of passive income lies in its promise of financial freedom, flexibility, and the potential for exponential growth. By pursuing passive income streams, individuals can build their own wealth-generating machines that allow them to lead the lives they desire. While passive income does require initial effort and ongoing management, the rewards can be life-changing. It's essential to remember that there is no one-size-fits-all approach, and individuals must explore their options and invest in strategies that align with their skills, resources, and long-term goals. As you embark on your journey, remember that passive income is a marathon, not a sprint, so be patient, stay focused, and let the magic of passive income transform your financial future.

Assessing Your Entrepreneurial Mindset

In today's rapidly changing business landscape, having an entrepreneurial mindset is more crucial than ever. It is not limited to those who start their own businesses; an entrepreneurial mindset is a valuable asset for anyone looking to excel in their career or make a meaningful impact in the world. This chapter aims to explore the key aspects of assessing your entrepreneurial mindset and provide you with practical insights to develop and nurture it further.

1. Understanding the Entrepreneurial Mindset:

The entrepreneurial mindset is a unique way of thinking and approaching challenges. It encompasses a combination of traits, attitudes, and behaviors that drive individuals to identify opportunities, take calculated risks, innovate, and persist despite obstacles. It goes beyond just being a successful businessperson; it is a mindset that can be applied to any domain of life.

2. The Pillars of an Entrepreneurial Mindset:

a) Creativity and Innovation:

Entrepreneurs possess the ability to think outside the box, finding unique solutions to problems and identifying opportunities others may overlook. Nurturing your creativity through lateral thinking, brainstorming, and embracing diverse perspectives can help foster an entrepreneurial mindset.

b) Risk-Taking and Resilience:

Taking risks is an inherent part of entrepreneurship, and a willingness to face the unknown is crucial. Entrepreneurs embrace failures as learning opportunities, bounce back from setbacks, and continually adapt their strategies. Building resilience by learning from failures, accepting constructive criticism, and managing stress can cultivate a robust entrepreneurial mindset.

c) Proactivity and Initiative:

Having a proactive approach to problem-solving and seizing opportunities is vital. Entrepreneurs are self-starters who take initiative, seek out possibilities, and actively engage in shaping their desired outcomes. Developing proactive habits, setting clear goals, and continuously challenging yourself are foundational to an entrepreneurial mindset.

d) Visionary Thinking:

Entrepreneurs have a clear vision of what they want to achieve and can visualize the path to success. Being able to set compelling goals, aligning actions, and communicating a vision to inspire others are integral aspects of the entrepreneurial mindset. Regularly reflecting on your goals, seeking feedback, and realigning your actions with your vision can help foster a strong sense of purpose.

3. Assessing Your Entrepreneurial Mindset:

To assess and understand your entrepreneurial mindset, it is important to reflect on your thoughts, behaviors, and actions. Consider the following aspects:

a) Self-Awareness:
Understanding your strengths, weaknesses, values, and motivations is the foundation for personal growth. Reflect on your past experiences, achievements, and challenges to gain insights into your entrepreneurial potential. Seeking feedback from mentors or trusted individuals can provide valuable perspectives on areas for improvement.

b) Comfort Zone Evaluation:
Entrepreneurs thrive outside their comfort zones, embracing new challenges and uncertainty. Assess your willingness to take risks, adaptability to change, and comfort with stepping into the unknown. Identify areas where you tend to stay within your comfort zone and challenge yourself to explore new territories.

c) Problem-Solving Skills:
Entrepreneurs tackle complex problems head-on and find innovative solutions. Evaluate your problem-solving skills, how you approach challenges, and your ability to think critically. Enhancing your problem-solving abilities through continuous learning, staying well-informed, and seeking diverse perspectives can nurture your entrepreneurial mindset.

d) Initiative and Action-Taking:

Entrepreneurs are action-oriented individuals who take the initiative and implement their ideas. Assess your ability to take calculated risks, seize opportunities, and make things happen. Identify instances where you may have held back and develop strategies to cultivate a bias towards action.

e) Resilience and Adaptability:

The entrepreneurial journey is filled with ups and downs, requiring resilience and adaptability. Reflect on how you handle failures, setbacks, and uncertainties. Assess your ability to bounce back, learn from failures, and adapt your strategies. Embracing challenges, seeking support when needed, and developing a growth mindset can enhance your resilience.

4. Developing and Nurturing Your Entrepreneurial Mindset:

Assessing your entrepreneurial mindset is just the beginning. To develop and nurture it further, consider the following strategies:

a) Continuous Learning:

Entrepreneurs are lifelong learners, continuously seeking knowledge and developing new skills. Embrace a growth mindset, pursue learning opportunities, and stay updated with industry trends. Engage in networking events, attend seminars, and leverage online platforms to broaden your knowledge base.

b) Building a Supportive Network:

Surrounding yourself with like-minded individuals can provide opportunities for collaboration, feedback, and support. Join entrepreneurial communities, seek out mentors, and collaborate with others to nurture your mindset. Engaging in meaningful discussions, sharing insights, and learning from fellow entrepreneurs can fuel your entrepreneurial spirit.

c) Embracing Failure:

Failures are an inevitable part of entrepreneurial endeavors. Embrace failures as learning experiences and opportunities for growth. Adopt a positive mindset towards failure, seek lessons from setbacks, and apply those insights to future ventures. The willingness to take risks and learn from failures is a hallmark of an entrepreneurial mindset.

d) Challenging Your Assumptions:

Examine your assumptions and challenge the status quo. Embrace curiosity, ask critical questions, and seek alternative perspectives. By breaking through limited thinking patterns, you can uncover new possibilities and foster an entrepreneurial mindset.

e) Setting and Realigning Goals:

Establish clear, measurable goals aligned with your vision. Regularly evaluate your progress, celebrate milestones, and realign your actions as necessary. Engaging in strategic planning, using SMART goals, and seeking feedback can help you stay on track.

Assessing and developing your entrepreneurial mindset requires ongoing effort and self-reflection. By embracing the pillars of the entrepreneurial mindset, assessing your strengths and weaknesses, and adopting strategies for growth, you can unlock your full entrepreneurial potential. Remember, an entrepreneurial mindset is not limited to starting a business; it is a mindset that empowers you to approach challenges with creativity, resilience, and an unwavering commitment to making a difference.

Calculating Initial Investment Requirements

In today's fast-paced world, vending machines have become an integral part of our lives, providing convenient access to snacks, beverages, and other essential products 24/7. Their widespread presence in public spaces, offices, and schools makes them a lucrative business opportunity for aspiring entrepreneurs. However, before delving into the vending machine industry, one must carefully calculate the initial investment requirements to ensure a successful and profitable venture. In this chapter, we will explore the various factors to consider when determining the investment needed for setting up a vending machine business.

1. Choosing the Right Machine:

The first and foremost step in calculating the initial investment requirements is selecting the appropriate vending machine. Choices range from traditional snack and drink machines to more specialized options like coffee machines, fresh food machines, or even custom-made machines catering to specific consumer needs. Each machine type has its own set of costs and considerations, such as maintenance, inventory storage, and electricity consumption. Careful research and market analysis are vital to understand the target customers and select the machine that aligns with their preferences.

2. Machine Acquisition Costs:

Once the type of machine is determined, the next step is evaluating its acquisition cost. The price of vending machines can vary greatly depending on factors such as size, capacity, durability, and additional features. Generally, new machines are more expensive than used ones, but they offer reliability and warranty. Used machines, on the other hand, can provide cost savings, but potential maintenance issues and shorter lifespan should be taken into account. It is essential to explore various suppliers, compare prices, and consider long-term benefits to make an informed decision.

3. Location

One of the critical factors influencing the success of a vending machine business is the strategic placement of machines. The right location can significantly impact customer footfall and sales volume. However, securing prime locations often involves costs like commission fees, rent, or profit-sharing agreements with the location owners. Assessing the target demographic, foot traffic, and competition in potential locations is essential to estimate or negotiate the associated expenses accurately.

4. Inventory and Product Costs:

The products stocked in the vending machine are the lifeblood of the business. Calculating the initial investment requires considering the cost of purchasing the initial inventory or stock. This includes snacks, beverages, or any other items that the vending machine will dispense. Suppliers offer various pricing options and discounts based on volume or exclusivity agreements. Estimating the inventory cost is crucial for pricing calculations and ensuring an optimal profit margin.

5. Machine Maintenance and Repair:

Like any other mechanical equipment, vending machines require regular maintenance and occasional repairs. It is crucial to account for these costs when determining the initial investment. Routine maintenance, such as cleaning, restocking, and testing, can be done by the business owner or an appointed employee. However, more complex repairs might necessitate hiring a professional technician or entering into a service agreement with a maintenance company. Evaluating the expected maintenance frequency and associated expenses is vital to avoid unexpected costs.

6. Operating Expenses:

Apart from the upfront costs, it is crucial to consider the ongoing operating expenses of a vending machine business. These expenses include utility bills, product restocking, transportation, insurance, and any additional fees or permits required for operating in specific locations. Reliable estimates should be made based on research, historical data, and potential future increases in costs. Budgeting for these expenses ensures efficient operations and avoids unforeseen financial burdens.

7. Cash Flow and Pricing Strategy:

Understanding the cash flow dynamics of the vending machine business is indispensable for calculating the initial investment requirements. Cash flow is determined by both sales revenue and costs, with the latter including inventory purchase, machine maintenance, location expenses, and various operational costs. The pricing strategy adopted plays a significant role in maximizing profits and ensuring sufficient returns on investment. Analyzing competitors' pricing, consumer expectations, and understanding the desired profit margin are essential steps to develop an effective pricing strategy.

8. Additional Considerations:

While calculating the initial investment requirements, certain additional factors should not be overlooked. These could include business registration and licensing fees, initial marketing and promotional costs, accounting and software expenses, and funds allocated for contingencies. Carefully assessing all aspects of the business journey will ensure a comprehensive financial plan, minimizing surprises and unforeseen expenses.

Determining the initial investment requirements for a vending machine business demands a holistic approach, considering various factors such as machine selection, acquisition costs, location expenses, inventory, maintenance, and ongoing operational costs. By conducting detailed market analysis and diligently estimating expenses, entrepreneurs can make informed decisions and establish a solid foundation for a successful venture.

Choosing the Right Vending Machine Types

Vending machines have become an integral part of our daily lives, offering convenience and accessibility for a wide range of products. From your favorite snacks and beverages to essential items like toiletries and electronics, vending machines have revolutionized the way we shop on-the-go. With so many options available in the market today, choosing the right vending machine type can be a daunting task. In this chapter, we will explore the various factors to consider when selecting vending machines for your business, ensuring optimal customer satisfaction and profitability.

1. Understanding Vending Machine Types:

Before diving into the selection process, it is crucial to understand the different types of vending machines available. While the basic concept remains the same—an automated machine dispensing products—a variety of models cater to specific needs. Some common vending machine types include:

a) Snack and Drink Machines: These traditional vending machines offer a wide selection of snacks, candies, and beverages. They are often found in offices, schools, and public places, providing quick and convenient refreshments.

b) Combo Machines: As the name suggests, combo machines combine snack and drink functionalities within a single unit. These versatile vending machines are popular in high-traffic locations as they offer a diverse range of products.

c) Coffee and Hot Beverage Machines: Ideal for coffee shops, gas stations, and waiting areas, these machines serve freshly brewed coffee, tea, hot chocolate, and other hot beverages. They are appreciated for their convenience, speed, and consistent quality.

d) Fresh Food Machines: These machines have gained popularity in recent years with the growing demand for healthier on-the-go meals. Fresh food vending machines provide a variety of sandwiches, salads, and other nutritious options.

e) Specialized Vending Machines: In addition to the above categories, there are specialized vending machines designed for specific products such as ice cream, cosmetics, electronics, and even artworks. These machines cater to a particular niche market and require careful consideration.

2. Analyzing Target Audience:

The success of a vending machine largely depends on understanding the target audience and tailoring the offerings accordingly. Consider the demographics, behavior patterns, and preferences of your potential customers. Are you targeting students in a university?

Employees in a corporate building? Travelers at an airport? Each group will have distinct requirements, and your vending machine selection should align with their needs.

3. Vending Machine Placement:

The placement of your vending machine is crucial to its success. High-traffic areas ensure a steady stream of potential customers, so analyze foot traffic patterns, such as entrances, hallways, waiting rooms, and common spaces. Consider factors such as accessibility, visibility, and convenience when finalizing the placement. Additionally, ensure that your chosen vending machine type is compatible with the available space without obstructing the flow.

4. Product Selection:

Once you have identified the target audience and chosen an appropriate vending machine type, it's time to curate the product selection. Analyze the demographics, preferences, and buying patterns of your target customers to offer a mix of popular and niche products that will attract their attention. Keep an eye on emerging trends and adapt to changing consumer demands. Regularly update and rotate the products to keep the offerings fresh and exciting, ensuring customer satisfaction and repeat business.

5. Payment Options:

In today's digital age, providing multiple payment options is essential. While cash is still widely used, it is crucial to accommodate mobile payments, credit cards, and contactless options to cater to a wider customer base. Choose vending machines that offer modern payment systems, ensuring that customers can make purchases conveniently and without hassle.

6. Maintenance and Support:

Proper maintenance and reliable support are crucial for the longevity and efficiency of your vending machines. Before making a purchase, research the manufacturer's reputation for customer service and after-sales support. Analyze warranty and maintenance agreements, as well as the availability of spare parts. A robust maintenance schedule will help minimize downtime and ensure uninterrupted service to your customers.

7. Energy Efficiency:

In today's environmentally conscious world, energy efficiency has become a significant consideration for businesses. Opt for vending machines that are equipped with energy-saving features, such as LED lighting, smart temperature control, and low-power modes. Not only will this reduce operating costs, but it will also contribute to a sustainable business model.

8. Security Features:

To protect your investment and ensure customer trust, select vending machines that incorporate robust security features. These can include tamper-proof mechanisms, secure coin and banknote validators, and surveillance systems. Additionally, consider vending machines with remote monitoring capabilities, allowing you to track sales, inventory levels, and maintenance requirements in real-time.

Selecting the right vending machine type is a critical decision that can impact both customer satisfaction and profitability. By understanding the different vending machine types available, analyzing the target audience, careful product selection, multiple payment options, maintenance and support, energy efficiency, and security features, you can ensure that your vending machine venture is a resounding success. Remember, choosing vending machines is only the first step, and continuous monitoring and optimization are paramount to building a thriving business.

Sourcing Suppliers and Machines

In the world of convenience and instant gratification, vending machines have become an indispensable part of our lives. Whether you crave a cold beverage on a scorching summer day or a quick snack during a busy day at work, these machines are always at your service. Behind the scenes, however, lies a complex process of sourcing suppliers and machines that keep these vending units running smoothly day in and day out. In this chapter, we will explore the intricacies of finding the right suppliers for your vending business and selecting the ideal machines to maximize profitability. So, let us embark on a journey through the world of vending machines and unravel the secrets of this industry.

Sourcing Suppliers for Your Vending Business

Before delving into the details of choosing the right vending machines, it is essential to establish reliable and efficient relationships with suppliers. These suppliers are the lifeline of your vending business, ensuring a constant supply of quality products to meet the demands of your customers. Here are some key steps to consider when sourcing suppliers for your vending machine venture:

1. Identify your product requirements: Begin by determining the product categories you wish to offer through your vending machines.

Whether it is beverages, snacks, healthy options, or a combination of these, clearly defining your product requirements will help you narrow down potential suppliers.

2. Research and evaluate suppliers: Conduct thorough market research to identify potential suppliers who are specialized in the products you seek. Consider factors such as product range, delivery capabilities, pricing, reliability, and reputation. Look for suppliers who can provide flexibility in meeting changing consumer preferences and trends.

3. Establish communication channels: Once you have identified potential suppliers, establish effective communication channels with them. This ensures smooth coordination and timely updates regarding product availability, pricing, and any other pertinent information.

4. Evaluate supplier performance: Regularly assess the performance of your suppliers based on factors such as product quality, on-time delivery, and responsiveness to issues or concerns. Keep an open line of communication to address any grievances or suggestions, fostering a mutually beneficial business relationship.

5. Seek supplier recommendations: Utilize networking opportunities within the vending machine industry to seek recommendations from experienced operators. Their insights can help guide you towards

reputable suppliers who have a proven track record of reliability and quality.

Selecting the Right Vending Machines

Once you have secured a reliable supplier network, the next crucial step is selecting the right vending machines for your business. The machines you choose will directly impact your operational efficiency, customer satisfaction, and ultimately, your profitability. Here are some factors to consider when selecting vending machines:

1. Determine machine type: Vending machines come in various forms, catering to different products and locations. Evaluate whether your target audience prefers refrigerated machines for beverages, snack machines, combination machines, coffee machines, or specialized options like fresh food vending machines. Consider the specific needs and preferences of your target market.

2. Analyze machine capacity: Assess the anticipated demand for your vending machines to choose the appropriate size and capacity. Factors such as footfall, location, and expected sales volume will influence the dimensions and internal configuration of the machines.

3. Consider machine features: Modern vending machines are equipped with various features and technologies that enhance user experience and operational efficiency. Look for features like cashless payment systems, touchscreens, advertising displays, remote

monitoring capabilities, and inventory tracking. Evaluate which features align with your business goals and customer expectations.

4. Evaluate maintenance requirements: Vending machines, like any mechanical device, require regular maintenance and occasional repairs. Consider the availability of spare parts and the ease of servicing when selecting machines. Opting for brands with a wide service network and comprehensive maintenance protocols can prevent prolonged downtime and minimize potential revenue loss.

5. Research machine manufacturers: Thoroughly research vending machine manufacturers to ensure you choose a reputable and established company. Look for manufacturers known for their quality craftsmanship, durable machines, and excellent customer support. Seek references and read reviews to gain insights into their track record and customer satisfaction levels.

Sourcing suppliers and selecting the right vending machines are pivotal elements in establishing a successful vending machine business. The quality of products and the efficiency of your machines directly influence customer satisfaction and, consequently, your financial success. By following the steps outlined in this chapter, you will be well-equipped to forge strong relationships with suppliers, choose the perfect vending machines, and provide a seamless experience for your customers. Remember, a well-stocked and well-maintained vending machine can be a true profit generator, ensuring that that thirst-quenching beverage or savory snack is just a button press away.

Navigating the Capital Investment Process

In today's fast-paced world, vending machines have become an integral part of our daily lives. Found in schools, hospitals, office buildings, and even on street corners, these machines provide us with quick and convenient access to snacks, beverages, and other essential items. Behind the scenes, however, lies a complex capital investment process that enables the existence of these ubiquitous machines. This chapter aims to shed light on the intricate journey of navigating the capital investment process for vending machines.

Identifying the Need

Any successful venture begins with identifying a need. When it comes to vending machines, entrepreneurs and businesses typically conduct extensive research to determine if there is sufficient demand for their products in a given location. Factors such as foot traffic, customer preferences, and existing competitors are considered during this phase.

Challenges may arise in identifying the right location. Local regulations, market saturation, and demographic analysis must be examined to ensure optimal placement. Additionally, businesses must be mindful of costs associated with securing a lease or ownership of the space where the vending machine will be located.

Capital Budgeting and Financial Planning

Once a need for a vending machine has been identified, the next step is to prepare a comprehensive capital budget and devise a financial plan. This involves forecasting the project costs, potential revenue streams, and the expected return on investment (ROI).

Project costs include the purchase or lease of the vending machine, installation expenses, maintenance and operational costs, and the cost of restocking inventory. Financial planners must also consider factors such as insurance coverage, taxes, and contingency funds to cover any unforeseen circumstances.

Furthermore, financial planners need to analyze the potential revenue streams. This involves estimating the expected sales volume, pricing strategy, and the gross margins. Thorough market research is essential to determine the average purchasing behavior, demographic trends, and the popular products within the target location.

Funding Options

After outlining the budget and financial plan, businesses need to explore various funding options. This may involve utilizing internal capital, seeking external investors, or obtaining loans from financial institutions.

Internal capital can be obtained through the business's retained earnings, cash reserves, or through reallocation of funds from other projects. However, this approach may limit the budget available for other business activities or require substantial financial sacrifices.

Alternatively, businesses can seek external investors to provide the necessary capital. This may involve presenting a compelling business plan, showcasing the potential for high returns, and demonstrating the expertise of the management team. In return, investors may expect equity or a share of future profits.

Another common funding option is securing a loan from a financial institution. In this case, businesses must present a solid business plan, including a repayment strategy, collateral, and a convincing case for the viability and profitability of the venture. It is crucial to carefully evaluate the terms and interest rates offered by different lenders to ensure they align with the financial plan and long-term objectives.

Procurement and Installation

Once the necessary funds have been secured, the procurement and installation phase comes into play. Businesses need to identify reputable suppliers or manufacturers of vending machines, ensuring they meet their desired specifications and offer competitive pricing.

After selecting the appropriate vendor, placing the order, and finalizing the purchase agreement, the installation process can begin. This involves coordinating with the supplier, logistics providers, and any involved contractors to ensure a smooth and timely installation. Businesses must also obtain the necessary permits and comply with regulatory requirements during this phase.

Operational Considerations

With the vending machine successfully installed, operational considerations take center stage. Management must develop comprehensive procedures and protocols for the day-to-day running of the machine, including maintenance, restocking, and cash management.

Maintenance involves routine checks, cleaning, and repairs to ensure the machine remains in optimal condition. Regular inspections from qualified technicians and a documented maintenance schedule are crucial to prevent equipment failure and minimize downtime.

Restocking is another critical aspect of operation. Businesses must establish reliable supply chains and maintain inventory levels to avoid stockouts or stale products. Analyzing sales data and customer preferences can assist in adjusting the product mix and optimizing stocking strategies.

Additionally, robust cash management practices should be implemented to safeguard cash flow, prevent theft, and reconcile transactions accurately. Deploying technology, such as cashless payment systems and real-time reporting, can streamline cash management processes and improve efficiency.

Marketing and Promotion

To maximize the success of a vending machine, marketing and promotion play a vital role. Businesses must develop marketing strategies to draw attention, differentiate themselves from competitors, and attract customers. This can be achieved through methods like signage, attractive packaging, loyalty programs, and innovative marketing campaigns.

Data analytics can be leveraged to gain insights into customer behavior, preferences, and response to promotional efforts. Armed with this information, businesses can refine their marketing strategies, optimize product offerings, and tailor promotions to specific customer segments.

Evaluating Performance and Continuous Improvement

Once a vending machine is operational, businesses must continuously evaluate its performance against the established financial targets. This involves monitoring sales volume, analyzing profitability, comparing actual versus projected costs, and assessing customer satisfaction.

Based on the performance evaluation, management can identify areas for improvement and implement necessary adjustments to drive profitability and enhance customer experience. This could include exploring new product offerings, renegotiating supplier contracts to reduce costs, implementing energy-efficient equipment, or expanding to new locations.

Navigating the capital investment process for a vending machine is a complex endeavor that requires careful planning, financial acumen, marketing expertise, and operational excellence. By identifying the need, preparing a comprehensive financial plan, securing funding, procuring and installing the machine, implementing operational strategies, and continuously evaluating performance, businesses can maximize the potential and profitability of their vending machines.

This chapter has provided an overview of the various stages involved in navigating the capital investment process for vending machines. While this process may vary depending on the specific circumstances, understanding these fundamental components is essential for any entrepreneur or business seeking to venture into the world of vending machines.

Chapter 2: Blueprinting Your Venture: Strategically Setting Up Your Vending Machines

In this chapter, we will explore the crucial process of strategically setting up your vending machines. The success of your venture greatly depends on the careful planning and execution of this step. Just like any other business, a vending machine operation requires a well-thought-out blueprint to ensure smooth operations, profitability, and customer satisfaction. We will delve into various aspects, including location selection, product assortment, machine placement, maintenance strategies, and maximizing profits. Let's dive in and discover the essential elements of setting up your vending machine venture.

Selecting Locations:

The adage "location, location, location" holds immense significance in the vending machine industry. Identifying the right locations for your machines is vital to maximize sales and profitability. Several factors come into play when selecting a suitable location:

1. Foot Traffic: Look for areas with high foot traffic, such as shopping centers, airports, schools, hospitals, and office complexes. These locations provide a steady stream of potential customers.

2. Target Audience: Consider the demographics of your target market and locate your machines accordingly. For instance, if your target audience is college students, placing machines near universities or college campuses would be ideal.

3. Competition: Analyze the competition in the area. While some level of competition is healthy, make sure you choose locations where there is a gap in the market or an opportunity to offer unique products or services.

4. Regulations: Familiarize yourself with local regulations regarding vending machines, permits, and licenses. Compliance with legal requirements is crucial to avoid unnecessary fines or legal issues.

Product Assortment:

Offering the right mix of products in your vending machines is key to attracting and retaining customers. Conduct thorough market research to determine the preferences and demands of your target audience. Consider the following factors when selecting your product assortment:

1. Variety: Offer a diverse range of products that caters to different

tastes and preferences. Include snacks, beverages, healthy options, and popular brands to cater to a wide customer base.

2. Seasonal Products: Adapt your product assortment to align with seasonal trends. For example, during the summer, introduce cold beverages and ice cream, while warm drinks and comfort foods could be popular during the winter season.

3. Healthy Options: In recent years, there has been a significant shift towards healthier eating habits. Include nutritious snacks, organic options, and gluten-free products to cater to health-conscious consumers.

4. Local Preferences: Consider local tastes and preferences when selecting your product assortment. Conduct surveys or engage with customers to understand their preferences and adjust your offerings accordingly.

Machine Placement:

Strategic placement of vending machines can increase customer visibility, convenience, and ultimately, sales. Pay attention to the following aspects while deciding on your machine placement:

1. High Traffic Areas: Position your machines in prominent areas with high visibility and constant foot traffic. Placing machines near entrances, lobbies, or waiting areas can significantly boost sales.

2. Optimal Accessibility: Ensure that your machines are easily accessible to customers, especially those with disabilities. Comply with accessibility guidelines to make your business more inclusive.

3. Synergistic Partnerships: Collaborate with complementary

businesses to create mutually beneficial partnerships. Placing vending machines in locations that align with your brand values or target audience can increase exposure and generate more sales.

Maintenance Strategies:

Maintaining and servicing your vending machines is vital for their longevity, efficiency, and customer satisfaction. Implement the following maintenance strategies to ensure smooth operations:

1. Regular Cleaning: Clean and sanitize your machines at regular intervals to uphold a hygienic environment. Display clear instructions on machine usage and cleanliness to encourage customer awareness.

2. Inventory Management: Maintain a systematic inventory management system to avoid stockouts or stale products. Regularly monitor sales data and adjust product assortments based on popularity.

3. Equipment Maintenance: Schedule routine maintenance checks to identify and address any potential issues promptly. Regularly inspect machine components such as coin mechanisms, bill acceptors, and temperature controls to ensure optimal functionality.

Maximizing Profits:

While setting up your vending machine venture, it's crucial to focus on maximizing profits. Explore strategies that will help you achieve higher returns on investment:

1. Pricing Strategies: Determine competitive yet profitable pricing for your products. Consider cost of goods, market demand, and

consumer willingness to pay when setting prices. Special promotions or loyalty programs can also attract customers and increase sales.

2. Dynamic Product Mix: Continuously analyze sales patterns and refine your product assortment accordingly. Remove slow-selling items and replace them with popular alternatives to maximize revenue.

3. Efficient Route Planning: Develop an optimal route plan for restocking and servicing your machines. Minimize travel distances between locations to reduce fuel costs and maximize time efficiency.

4. Technology Integration: Embrace technology to streamline operations and enhance customer experience. Adopt cashless payment options, implement remote monitoring systems, and leverage analytics to make data-driven decisions.

Setting up your vending machine venture requires careful planning, attention to detail, and a customer-centric approach. The blueprinting process involves selecting the right locations, curating an attractive product assortment, strategically placing machines, implementing effective maintenance strategies, and focusing on maximizing profits. By following the guidelines in this chapter, you will be well on your way to creating a successful and profitable vending machine business. Remember, your dedication and continuous improvement are crucial for long-term success in this competitive industry.

Deciding on Product Selection: Snacks, Beverages, or Specialties

In the competitive world of retail, one of the most critical decisions managers face is selecting the right mix of products to offer. The product selection plays a pivotal role in attracting and retaining customers, driving sales, and ultimately determining the success of a retail establishment. This chapter delves into the three main categories of products – snacks, beverages, and specialties – and explores the factors to consider when making decisions in this domain.

The Importance of Product Selection:

Before delving into the intricacies of choosing between snacks, beverages, or specialties, it is crucial to understand why product selection is paramount. An effective selection not only targets the desires and preferences of the target audience but also sets the store apart from its competitors. A well-curated collection of products can define a brand, create a memorable shopping experience, and ultimately boost sales. The selection process involves meticulous research, industry analysis, and staying in tune with consumer trends.

1. Snacks:

Snacks are a widely popular product category that caters to people's cravings and provides an instant source of pleasure and satisfaction. From traditional potato chips to healthier alternatives like granola bars, snacks come in a variety of forms and flavors. When deciding on including snacks in the product mix, several factors need to be taken into consideration.

1.1 Consumer Demographics and Preferences:
Understanding the target audience is paramount to selecting the right snacks. Age group, dietary preferences, and cultural background influence snack choices. For example, a store in a predominantly young and health-conscious neighborhood might favor organic and plant-based snacks, while a store located near a university campus could benefit from offering a wider range of affordable, portable snacks suitable for students.

1.2 Brand Reputation and Awareness:
Since snacks are often impulse purchases, brand reputation plays a critical role in the selection process. Recognizable, trusted brands like Doritos or Nature Valley will attract customers and instill confidence in the quality of the snacks offered. However, it is also valuable to incorporate emerging and local brands to appeal to customers seeking unique or artisanal products.

1.3 Seasonality and Trends:
Snack preferences can vary by season, with certain treats being more

popular during specific times of the year. By staying attuned to current trends and seasonal demands, retailers can capitalize on consumer interest. For example, offering pumpkin spice-flavored snacks during autumn or stocking up on heart-shaped chocolates for Valentine's Day can drive sales and create a sense of relevance.

2. Beverages:

The beverage category encompasses a broad range of products, from carbonated drinks to coffee, tea, and alcohol. Deciding on the inclusion of beverages in the product mix involves careful consideration of the following factors.

2.1 Target Market and Lifestyle:

Similar to snacks, understanding the target market and their lifestyle is crucial when selecting beverages to offer. For instance, a store located in a busy urban area might benefit from stocking a diverse selection of ready-to-drink coffee and energy drinks to cater to the fast-paced, convenience-oriented lifestyle of its customers. On the other hand, a store situated in a suburban neighborhood may prioritize a well-rounded collection of coffee, tea, and juices to accommodate the preferences of families and health-conscious individuals.

2.2 Beverages as Complementary Products:

Beverages often serve as complementary products to other items, such as snacks or sandwiches. Retailers should consider how well beverages align with their existing selection and enhance the overall shopping experience. For example, offering a variety of specialty coffees to accompany freshly baked pastries can elevate the convenience and ambiance of a store. On the flip side, a mismatched beverage choice could detract from the customer's experience and reduce the likelihood of repeat visits.

2.3 Health and Wellness Trends:
The growing focus on health and wellness has significantly influenced the beverage industry. Consumers are increasingly seeking drinks that offer functional benefits, such as hydration, natural ingredients, or specific nutrients. Retailers should remain aware of these trends and incorporate healthier beverage options, such as kombucha, cold-pressed juices, or low-sugar alternatives. This not only caters to evolving consumer preferences but also positions the store as a champion of healthy lifestyles.

3. Specialties:

Specialty products refer to a unique, niche selection that sets the store apart from its competitors. These products are often distinguished by their exclusivity, craftsmanship, or cultural significance. Considerations when deciding on incorporating specialties include:

3.1 Uniqueness and Differentiation:
Specialty products provide an opportunity for retailers to differentiate themselves from larger, mainstream competitors. These items often possess a story, craftsmanship, or rarity that captivates

customers and creates an elevated shopping experience. Whether it's handicrafts, artisanal food products, or a curated collection of rare teas, specialties should highlight the store's character and values.

3.2 Utilizing Local or Regional Products:

Embracing local or regional specialties offers several advantages. It fosters a sense of community, supports local businesses, and provides customers with items they may not find elsewhere. In many cases, these products have a cultural or historical significance tied to a particular region, enticing both locals and tourists alike. By aligning the specialties with the store's location, retailers can tap into the desire for authentic and unique products.

3.3 Testing and Evaluating:

While incorporating specialties can define a store's identity, it is important to test their reception and evaluate customer feedback. Specialty products often cater to niche markets, and there can be varying degrees of demand. Conducting surveys and gathering customer insights can help refine the selection, ensuring the right balance between exclusivity and market appeal.

Deciding on the product selection within the categories of snacks, beverages, or specialties is a crucial task that demands meticulous research, understanding of consumer preferences, and adaptation to industry trends. By carefully considering various factors such as target market, brand awareness, lifestyle, seasonality, uniqueness, and regional relevance, retailers can create a compelling mix of products that cater to their customers' desires, differentiate themselves from competitors, and foster a memorable shopping experience.

Optimal Pricing Strategies for Maximum Returns

Vending machines have become an integral part of our everyday lives. From office break rooms and shopping malls to train stations and airports, these self-service devices are ubiquitous and provide convenient access to an assortment of products and services. However, the success of a vending machine business relies heavily on the pricing strategy implemented. In this chapter, we will explore the various factors that influence optimal pricing strategies for maximizing returns in vending machines.

Understanding Consumer Behavior

Before delving into pricing strategies, it is crucial to understand consumer behavior and the factors that influence their purchasing decisions. Several key elements play a vital role in determining consumer behavior when using vending machines:

1. Convenience: Vending machines are designed to provide quick and easy access to products. Consumers value the convenience factor greatly, especially when they are in a hurry or have limited options available.

2. Impulse Buying: Vending machines are known to trigger impulse buying. Consumers tend to make spontaneous purchasing decisions,

often driven by enticing product displays and appealing packaging.

3. Price Sensitivity: Consumers are generally price-sensitive when using vending machines. They expect fair pricing that aligns with the perceived value of the product being offered.

4. Perception of Quality: The perceived quality of products sold in vending machines can influence purchasing decisions. Consumers often associate higher prices with better quality and are more willing to pay a premium for perceived value.

Factors Affecting Pricing Strategies

When determining the optimal pricing strategy for a vending machine, several factors must be considered to maximize returns:

1. Product Cost and Markup: A crucial aspect of pricing strategy is understanding the cost of the products being sold. This includes both the wholesale price and any additional costs incurred, such as stocking and maintenance. Applying a reasonable markup is essential to generate profits.

2. Competition: Vending machines often face competition from nearby establishments, such as convenience stores or cafes. Understanding the pricing strategies employed by the competition is vital to ensure competitiveness and avoid overpricing.

3. Target Market: Identifying the target market is critical in establishing the optimal pricing strategy. Different demographics have varying purchasing power and willingness to pay. Understanding the income levels, preferences, and habits of the target market allows for tailored pricing strategies.

4. Location: The location of a vending machine plays a pivotal role in determining price optimization. High-traffic areas with captive audiences, such as airports or hospitals, may allow for higher prices due to the convenience factor. In contrast, lower footfall locations necessitate more competitive pricing to drive sales.

Pricing Strategies for Vending Machines

1. Cost-plus Pricing: This method involves determining the total cost of product acquisition and then adding a fixed percentage or amount as profit. Cost-plus pricing offers a straightforward approach to ensure profit margins while retaining flexibility for adjustments over time.

2. Penetration Pricing: This strategy focuses on setting initial prices lower than competitors to capture a larger market share quickly. Penetration pricing aims to build customer loyalty and drive repeat purchases. However, it may require careful monitoring and price adjustments to maintain profitability over the long term.

3. Psychological Pricing: This approach involves employing pricing

techniques that leverage consumers' emotional response to specific price points. For example, setting prices just below a round number (e.g., $4.99 instead of $5.00) can create the perception of a better deal and stimulate impulse buying.

4. Dynamic Pricing: Utilizing advanced technologies, dynamic pricing allows for real-time adjustments based on demand and other factors. By integrating machine learning algorithms and data analysis, vending machines can ensure optimal pricing throughout the day, adapting to peak periods and seasonal variations.

5. Bundling: Bundling products together at a discounted price can stimulate sales by offering consumers a perceived value proposition. For instance, offering a combo deal with a snack and a beverage at a lower combined price can entice consumers to spend more, resulting in increased overall revenue.

Implementing and Evaluating Pricing Strategies

Implementing and evaluating the effectiveness of pricing strategies involves continuous monitoring and analysis. This process can be facilitated through the use of technology, such as vending machine management systems, which provide real-time data on sales, trends, and consumer behavior. Analyzing this information can help identify patterns, optimize prices, and make informed decisions.

Additionally, customer feedback and surveys can provide valuable insights into how pricing impacts the perceived value of products and the overall customer experience. Listening to consumer preferences and adjusting pricing accordingly can lead to improved customer satisfaction and enhanced returns.

Optimal pricing strategies are essential for maximizing returns in vending machines. By understanding consumer behavior, factors affecting pricing, and employing appropriate pricing strategies, vending machine businesses can strike a balance between profitability and customer satisfaction. Regular evaluation and adaptation of pricing strategies based on data and customer feedback are crucial for long-term success in this highly competitive industry.

Designing Eye-catching Machines and Displays

In today's fast-paced world, vending machines have become a ubiquitous presence, catering to our needs for snacks, beverages, and various products at almost every corner. Amidst the sea of vending machines, how can you make yours stand out? How can you design eye-catching machines and displays that captivate potential customers and entice them to make a purchase? In this chapter, we will delve into the fascinating world of vending machine design, exploring various creative strategies and techniques that can elevate your vending machine's appearance to a whole new level.

Understanding the Importance of Eye-Catching Design:
Before we dive into the specifics of vending machine design, it is crucial to comprehend why eye-catching design matters. In a highly competitive market, where potential customers are bombarded with countless options, a visually appealing machine can make all the difference. An eye-catching design not only grabs attention but also leaves a lasting impression, potentially increasing customer engagement, sales, and brand loyalty.

The Role of Colors and Lighting:
One of the most fundamental aspects of designing an eye-catching vending machine is the use of colors and lighting. Colors have the power to evoke emotions, set moods, and communicate brand

values. Select a color scheme that aligns with your brand identity and resonates with your target audience. Bold and vibrant colors can create an energetic and playful atmosphere, attracting attention and creating a sense of excitement.

Moreover, integrating well-thought-out lighting can further enhance your machine's visual appeal. Subtle backlighting can draw attention to specific areas, highlighting products or promotional messages. LED lights can add a modern touch, making your machine stand out in dimly lit areas. Selecting the right combination of colors and lighting techniques ensures that your vending machine becomes a focal point in its surroundings.

Incorporating Innovative Materials:

A traditional vending machine design might blend into its environment, failing to grab the attention of passersby. However, by incorporating innovative materials, you can create a visually striking machine that sets itself apart. Experimenting with materials like glass, metal, wood, or even eco-friendly materials can add an element of uniqueness to your design.

For instance, using transparent sections or glass panels can give customers a glimpse of the products inside. This can pique their curiosity, encouraging them to approach and explore further. Incorporating metal accents or finishes can exude a sense of durability and quality. Introducing elements of natural wood can create a warm and inviting aesthetic, standing out amidst a sea of machines made from synthetic materials. By daring to deviate from the norm and embracing innovative materials, you can elevate your vending machine's visual appeal to new heights.

Leveraging Visual Branding:

Powerful branding is an essential element of any successful business, and vending machines are no exception. Consistently incorporating your brand's visual elements into your machine's design not only reinforces brand recognition but also creates a sense of trust and familiarity. This is particularly crucial for customers who have interacted with your brand before.

To create eye-catching displays for your vending machine, ensure that your brand colors, logos, and taglines are prominently displayed. Depending on your machine's size, you can also utilize vinyl wraps or graphical illustrations to tell a visual story that resonates with your target audience. Seamlessly integrating visual branding across all elements of your machine's display will not only catch the eye but also strengthen brand loyalty in the long run.

Interactive and Engaging Displays:

As technology continues to advance, leveraging interactive displays within vending machines has become an exciting opportunity to catch customers' attention. Engaging displays invite potential customers to interact with your machine, leaving a memorable experience that can lead to increased sales.

Consider incorporating touchscreens with interactive interfaces that allow users to browse products, find nutritional information, or even play mini-games for discounts. Interactive displays can also provide personalized recommendations based on user preferences, further enhancing customer engagement. Additionally, integrating motion sensors that trigger captivating visuals or interactive lighting can create a sense of novelty and excitement for passersby.

Promoting Seasonal and Limited-Time Offers:

Seasonal and limited-time offers are an effective marketing tool to create a sense of urgency and encourage customers to make a purchase. Vending machines can tap into this strategy by incorporating eye-catching displays that showcase these promotions. For example, during the festive season, you can decorate your machine with themed graphics, colors, and lighting to evoke a cheerful atmosphere and instill a sense of holiday spirit. Alternatively, for limited-time offers, consider incorporating countdown timers or dynamic elements to visually communicate the urgency of the promotion. By regularly refreshing your machine's design to reflect ongoing promotions, you can continuously capture the attention of potential customers.

Designing eye-catching machines and displays for vending machines is an art that involves a delicate balance of colors, materials, branding, interactivity, and promotional prowess. Your goal should be to create a visually captivating machine that not only promotes your products effectively but also leaves a lasting impression on customers. Through an innovative approach to design, a keen understanding of your target audience, and an unwavering commitment to powerful branding, your vending machine has the potential to become a magnet for customers, generating increased sales and brand recognition.

Ensuring Accessibility and User-Friendly Interfaces

In this digital era, vending machines have become an integral part of our daily lives. Whether it is a quick snack, a refreshing beverage, or even a technological gadget, vending machines offer convenience and accessibility around the clock. As the demand for these automated dispensers has increased, so has the need to ensure that they are accessible and offer user-friendly interfaces for individuals with diverse needs. This chapter delves into the importance of designing vending machines with accessibility in mind and touches upon some best practices to make them user-friendly.

Understanding Accessibility

Accessibility refers to the inclusive design of products and services that allow people of all abilities to access and use them easily. When it comes to vending machines, accessibility takes on a crucial role, as these machines are meant to cater to a wide range of users, including those with disabilities.

Various disabilities can affect individuals' ability to interact with vending machines, such as visual impairments, hearing impairments, cognitive impairments, and physical disabilities. Designing accessible vending machines requires understanding and considering the diverse needs of these users, ensuring that everyone can independently operate and interact with the machine.

Creating Accessible Vending Machines

1. Visual Accessibility

Visual impairments can make it difficult for users to read small text, distinguish colors, or perceive visual cues. To address these challenges, vending machines should incorporate features that aid visual accessibility:

a) Clear and readable text: The text used on the vending machine interface should be legible, using a large and easy-to-read font. Avoid using fancy or decorative fonts that can be challenging to decipher.

b) High color contrast: Use colors with high contrast to ensure that text and elements stand out clearly against the background. This helps users with low vision differentiate between different options and navigate the vending machine with ease.

c) Braille labels: Incorporating Braille labels alongside text instructions can greatly assist users with visual impairments. Braille labels should be placed strategically near the corresponding buttons or touchpoints.

2. Auditory Accessibility

Hearing impairments can make it challenging for individuals to perceive audio cues, alerts, or instructions. To enhance auditory accessibility, vending machines should consider the following:

a) Visual prompts: Accompany audio cues with visual prompts, such as flashing lights or on-screen animations, to ensure that users with hearing impairments are alerted to important information or messages.

b) Closed captioning: If the vending machine employs video or audio instructions, providing closed captioning or subtitles can enable individuals with hearing impairments to understand the content accurately.

3. Cognitive Accessibility

Cognitive impairments may affect users' memory, attention span, or ability to process information quickly. Designing vending machines to be cognitively accessible involves simplifying the interface and minimizing the cognitive load. Here are some practices to consider:

a) Clear and concise instructions: Vending machines should provide straightforward and unambiguous instructions using simple language and avoiding technical jargon. Break down complex tasks into smaller, manageable steps.

b) Intuitive layout and navigation: The interface should have a logical and organized layout, minimizing distractions and ensuring that options and buttons are easy to locate. Use clear icons or symbols to represent different products or functions.

4. Physical Accessibility

Physical disabilities can affect users' fine motor skills, dexterity, or mobility, making it difficult to interact physically with traditional machines. Here are some ways to enhance physical accessibility:

a) Ergonomic design: Designing the vending machine with ergonomic considerations, such as reachable height, accommodating wheelchair access, and ensuring that buttons and touchpoints are easily operable by users with limited mobility.

b) Assistive devices and interfaces: Implementing assistive technologies like sip-and-puff interfaces, large tactile buttons, or touchscreens with customizable layouts can significantly enhance the accessibility and usability for those with physical disabilities.

User-Friendly Interfaces

In addition to accessibility, vending machines should also strive to offer user-friendly interfaces for a seamless user experience. Consider the following factors to create a user-friendly vending machine:

1. Intuitive and Simple Interface

Users should be able to interact with the vending machine effortlessly, without any confusion or frustration. The interface should be intuitive, minimizing the learning curve and allowing users to operate the machine intuitively.

2. Clearly Labeled Options

Each option on the vending machine should be clearly labeled, indicating the product, quantity, price, and any other vital information. Users should easily find and identify their desired item without any ambiguity.

3. Quick and Efficient Transactions

Speed and efficiency are vital in vending machine interactions. Users expect a swift and hassle-free experience, so the interface should facilitate quick transactions, minimizing unnecessary steps or confirmation prompts.

4. Error Prevention and Recovery

Errors can occur during vending machine interactions, such as failed transactions, dispense errors, or incorrect change. The interface should be designed to prevent errors through clear instructions and confirmation prompts. Additionally, an intuitive error recovery process should be in place to guide users on how to resolve any issues they encounter.

Ensuring accessibility and user-friendly interfaces for vending machines is essential to foster inclusivity and convenience for all users.

By considering visual, auditory, cognitive, and physical accessibility, designers can create vending machines that cater to a diverse range of users. Simultaneously, user-friendly interfaces enhance the overall experience, minimizing confusion and maximizing usability.

Through inclusive design, vending machines can truly become accessible and intuitive tools that benefit everyone, regardless of abilities.

Chapter 3: Location, Location, Profits: Placing Your Vending Machines Strategically

In the world of vending machines, the importance of location cannot be overstated. A well-placed vending machine can be a cash cow, generating profits round the clock. On the other hand, a poorly situated machine can struggle to attract customers and barely break even. In this chapter, we will explore the art and science of strategically placing vending machines to maximize profits. We will delve into various factors to consider when selecting locations, discuss the key types of venues, and share invaluable tips for negotiating agreements with location owners. So hop on board as we embark on this exciting journey of mapping out lucrative locations for your vending machines!

Factors to Consider

Before we dive into the specifics of locating vending machines, it's essential to understand the factors that contribute to a profitable placement. By meticulously analyzing these variables, you can make informed decisions that will significantly impact your bottom line. Here are some key factors to consider:

1. Foot Traffic: The most crucial consideration when selecting a location is foot traffic. The more people passing by your machine, the higher the potential customer base. Busy streets, shopping malls, office buildings, and hospitals are prime examples of high-traffic locations.

2. Target Audience: Different venues cater to different demographics. Consider your target market and its preferences. If you're selling healthy snacks, a gym or a fitness center might be an ideal location. On the other hand, a school or a university might be a better fit for vending machines offering drinks and snacks popular with students.

3. Competitors: Keep an eye out for competing vending machines in your desired location. Analyze their offerings, pricing, and overall performance. Identifying gaps in the market can help you tailor your products and services accordingly to gain a competitive edge.

4. Accessibility: Convenience plays a significant role in attracting customers. Ensure that your machines are easily accessible and visible to passersby. Locations near entrances, common areas, waiting rooms, and break rooms tend to perform well.

5. Security: Consider the security of a potential location. Places with a higher risk of theft or damage might not be the best choice. Opt for well-lit, secure premises or install security measures like cameras and alarms to safeguard your investment.

Types of Venues

Now that we have explored the vital factors to consider, let's delve into the different types of venues where you can strategically place your vending machines:

1. Offices: Office buildings are a goldmine for vending machines. Employees frequent these locations throughout the day, creating a constant flow of potential customers. Consider placing machines in break rooms, cafeterias, or near meeting rooms to capture the attention of busy professionals.

2. Educational Institutions: Schools, colleges, and universities offer an excellent opportunity to cater to a large student population. Students often crave quick snacks and beverages between classes or during breaks, making educational institutions a highly profitable location.

3. Hospitals: Hospitals and healthcare facilities can be fertile ground for successful vending machine placement. Patients, visitors, and medical staff often seek refreshments during their time at the facility. Opt for high-traffic areas like lobbies, waiting rooms, or cafeterias to attract consistent patronage.

4. Leisure and Recreational Facilities: Gyms, sports centers, amusement parks, and entertainment venues are great locations for vending machines that offer health-conscious snacks and beverages.

Customers engaged in physical activities are more likely to appreciate and purchase such products.

5. Shopping Centers: Shopping malls and retail complexes guarantee high foot traffic throughout the day. Capitalize on this captive audience by placing vending machines near entrances, food courts, or popular stores. Customize your offerings to match the shopping preferences of your target audience to maximize sales.

Negotiating Agreements

Once you have identified potential locations, the next step is to secure agreements with location owners. Successful negotiations can make all the difference in the profitability of your vending machines. Here are some valuable tips to consider:

1. Understand the Owner's Perspective: Put yourself in the shoes of the location owner. Understand their motivations, concerns, and expectations. Align your proposal with their interests, highlighting the benefits they will derive from having a vending machine on their premises.

2. Present a Professional Image: Approach negotiations with a professional demeanor. Dress appropriately, be punctual, and prepare a well-organized presentation. Show the location owner that you take your business seriously and that you will be a reliable partner.

3. Research Market Rates: Before starting negotiations, research prevailing market rates for vending machine placement in similar venues. This knowledge will help you negotiate a fair and competitive agreement that is mutually beneficial.

4. Tailor Your Offer: Customize your proposal to fit the specific needs of the location owner. Offer incentives such as a percentage of sales, reduced commissions, or even free maintenance and restocking services. The more enticing your offer, the higher the likelihood of acceptance.

5. Communicate Clearly: Clearly articulate the benefits of having a vending machine at their location. Emphasize the convenience factor for the venue's patrons, potential increases in foot traffic, and the potential for additional revenue streams.

Strategic placement of vending machines is essential for maximizing profits. By carefully analyzing factors such as foot traffic, target audience, competition, accessibility, and security, you can make informed decisions about where to situate your machines. Consider venues such as offices, educational institutions, hospitals, recreational facilities, and shopping centers that align with your target market. Lastly, negotiate agreements that benefit both parties involved to ensure a successful and profitable venture. With a well-thought-out placement strategy and effective negotiation skills, your vending machines can become lucrative sources of continuous income. Now that you have grasped the fundamentals, it's time to hit the streets and explore the world of vending machine placement!

Unveiling the Art of Location Scouting

In the world of vending machines, success relies heavily on finding the perfect location. A well-chosen spot can be the difference between soaring profits and a disappointing venture. Location scouting requires an artistic approach, a blend of creativity, analytical thinking, and an understanding of consumer behavior. In this chapter, we delve into the intricacies of the art of location scouting for vending machines, uncovering the key factors to consider and the techniques to employ to maximize your chances of success.

1. Understanding the Psychology of Spaces:

Before embarking on any location scouting mission, it is crucial to grasp the psychology of spaces and how they interact with consumer behavior. People are influenced by their surroundings, sometimes even subconsciously, and this can greatly impact their decision-making process. For instance, a vending machine placed in a clean, well-lit, and aesthetically pleasing space will naturally attract more attention than one tucked away in a dimly lit corner. The ambiance, layout, and general atmosphere of the surroundings can either excite or deter potential customers.

2. Identifying Target Markets:

Once you have a firm grasp on the psychology of spaces, it is important to identify your target market. Who are your potential customers, and where can you find them? Determining the demographics and preferences of your target market will help narrow down your search for the perfect location. For example, if you are targeting a health-conscious crowd, consider placing your vending machine near gyms or yoga studios. On the other hand, if your target market is university students, explore opportunities near college campuses or student centers.

3. Foot Traffic Analysis:

Foot traffic analysis is a critical aspect of location scouting for vending machines. You want to position your machine in an area with high foot traffic to maximize exposure and potential sales. To conduct a thorough foot traffic analysis, begin by scouting potential locations during different days and times, noting the number of people passing by and their behavior. Additionally, consider the flow of foot traffic. Is it mainly one-way, or is there a circulation pattern that passes by your proposed location repeatedly? In crowded areas, proximity to major entry or exit points can make a significant difference.

4. Co-Location Opportunities:

Exploring co-location opportunities is an effective approach to location scouting for vending machines. Co-location involves aligning your machine with complementary businesses or services to create a symbiotic relationship. By identifying establishments that draw a similar target market, you can piggyback on their foot traffic and increase your chances of success. For example, placing a vending machine stocked with healthy snacks next to a gym can tap into the existing customer base and provide a convenient post-workout solution.

5. Competition Analysis:

Competition analysis is a key element often overlooked in location scouting for vending machines. Conduct thorough research to identify existing vending machines in your desired area. Map out their locations, the products they offer, and their pricing strategies. By understanding your competition, you can leverage their strengths and weaknesses to your advantage. If an area is already saturated with vending machines, consider offering a unique product range or targeting a niche market that is currently underserved.

6. Accessibility and Convenience:

Another vital factor to consider in location scouting is the accessibility and convenience of the chosen spot. Is there ample parking nearby? Is the machine easily visible and within reach? Can it be serviced and refilled without creating logistical nightmares? Ensuring convenience for both customers and operators fosters a positive experience, encouraging repeat visits and allowing for efficient maintenance.

7. Negotiating Partnerships:

In some cases, securing the ideal location for your vending machine may require negotiation and forging partnerships. Approach business owners who align with your target market and offer them a mutually beneficial proposition. For instance, offer a percentage of profits or revenue sharing to incentivize them to allow placement on their premises. Building strong partnerships not only secures prime locations but also increases the chances of success and longevity for both parties.

8. Adapting to Emerging Technologies:

While scouting for locations, it is crucial to stay up-to-date with emerging technologies that could enhance your location selection. Utilize mapping and data analysis tools to identify areas with high smartphone penetration, as this indicates potential tech-savvy customers. Additionally, explore the potential of incorporating cashless payment options and touchless interfaces to align with changing consumer preferences. Embracing technology will not only attract more customers but will give your vending machine a competitive edge.

Negotiating Win-Win Deals with Host Locations.

As the vending machine industry continues to grow, one crucial aspect of success lies in securing optimal locations for your machines. Choosing the right host locations can significantly impact your revenue and customer reach. However, gaining access to prime spots is often a challenging task that requires effective negotiation skills. In this chapter, we will explore the art of negotiating win-win deals with host locations, providing insights and strategies to help you establish fruitful partnerships.

Understanding the Importance of Strategic Locations

Before delving into negotiation techniques, it is paramount to comprehend why securing strategic locations is vital to your vending machine business's success. Prime locations offer several advantages, such as:

1. High foot traffic: Placing your vending machines in areas with a significant number of potential customers increases the probability of transactions. Malls, office buildings, schools, and transportation hubs are all excellent examples of such locations.
2. Target audience alignment: Selecting host locations that align with your target market ensures maximum profitability. For instance, placing healthy snack options in gyms or organic food vending

machines in wellness centers enhances customer satisfaction and boosts sales.

3. Visibility and accessibility: Vending machines placed in highly visible and accessible areas tend to attract more customers. Deploying machines near entrances, common areas, or heavily frequented spaces within host locations can be advantageous.

4. Convenience and time-saving: Providing customers with convenient access to snacks, beverages, or other products when they are away from traditional storefronts or dining areas can drive repeated sales.

Effective Preparation: Gathering Information

Before initiating any negotiations, thorough preparation is essential. Gathering detailed information about potential host locations helps in creating a solid foundation for approaching the negotiation process. The key information you should acquire includes:

1. Foot traffic and demographics: Determine the number of people passing through the potential location daily, as well as their demographics. Such information will allow you to assess whether the audience aligns with your target market and the potential reach of your vending machines.

2. Existing vending machines: Identify any competitors or existing

vending machines operating in the area. Understanding the competition will help you develop persuasive arguments and differentiate your proposal to the host location.

3. Host location objectives: Gain insights into the goals and objectives of the prospective host location. Determine how they aim to benefit from the partnership. By aligning your interests with theirs, you can present a more compelling case during negotiations.

Initiating Contact and Building Rapport

Once you have completed the preparation phase, it is time to initiate contact and build rapport with the decision-makers at the potential host locations. Here are some strategies to establish connections:

1. Personalized outreach: Rather than sending generic emails or letters, make an effort to personalize your communications. Address the recipient by their name and mention specific details about their location or potential benefits of a partnership.

2. Introduce your brand and value proposition: Clearly articulate why partnering with your vending machine business will be advantageous for the host location. Highlight your brand's unique selling points, such as high-quality products, innovative technology, or exceptional customer service.

3. Attend networking events: Participating in local business events

or industry-specific conferences can provide valuable opportunities to connect with potential host locations face-to-face. Building relationships in person often yields better negotiation outcomes.

Negotiation Strategies for Win-Win Deals

Negotiating win-win deals involves finding common ground and mutually beneficial solutions. Implement the following strategies to increase the likelihood of securing favorable agreements with host locations:

1. Understand their needs and concerns: Begin the negotiation process by actively listening to the needs and concerns of the host location. Demonstrating empathy and understanding will encourage open communication and facilitate a collaborative negotiation environment.

2. Showcase the benefits: Present a comprehensive proposal that outlines the advantages the host location can expect from having your vending machine(s) on their premises. Focus on how your machines can enhance their customers' experience, increase foot traffic, and generate additional revenue streams.

3. Offer incentives: To sweeten the deal, consider offering incentives to the host location. This could involve a percentage of revenue as a profit-sharing arrangement or extended warranty and maintenance services for the machines. Such incentives demonstrate your

commitment to building a long-term, mutually beneficial
relationship.

4. Flexibility and compromise: Negotiation is a give-and-take
process. Be willing to make concessions and find compromises that
benefit both parties. Flexibility can prove crucial in resolving
potential disagreements and reaching a mutually satisfying
agreement.

5. Long-term perspective: Emphasize the benefits of a long-term
partnership. Assure the host location that you are committed to their
success and offer strategies for ongoing collaboration, such as
regular maintenance, product rotation, or periodic marketing
campaigns to keep the vending machines attractive and engaging.

Understanding Foot Traffic and Demographics

If you have ever stepped foot inside a bustling shopping mall or strolled along a busy city street, you have witnessed foot traffic in action. Foot traffic refers to the movement of people on foot in a given area, and it plays a vital role in shaping the dynamics of businesses and communities. By understanding foot traffic patterns and analyzing the demographics of those who traverse these paths, we can unlock valuable insights that can inform strategic decisions for various stakeholders.

1.1 The Power of Foot Traffic

Foot traffic analysis is an essential tool for businesses seeking to maximize their profitability. By monitoring foot traffic patterns, retailers can gain a deeper understanding of customer behavior, preferences, and purchasing habits. This knowledge allows them to optimize store layouts, product displays, and marketing strategies to attract and retain customers.

Similarly, city planners and urban developers rely on foot traffic analysis to design functional and appealing public spaces. By evaluating foot traffic patterns, planners can identify areas of congestion and allocate resources accordingly. This knowledge enables them to enhance the pedestrian experience, foster community engagement, and promote economic growth.

1.2 The Role of Demographics

Demographics, on the other hand, provide invaluable information about the characteristics of individuals who comprise foot traffic. Understanding the demographic composition of foot traffic helps businesses tailor their offerings to meet the needs and preferences of their target market segments. Additionally, demographics aid city planners in identifying specific groups that frequent certain areas, allowing for the implementation of policies and infrastructure improvements that cater to those populations.

Measuring and Analyzing Foot Traffic

Now that we have established the significance of foot traffic and demographics, let us delve into the methods and tools employed to measure and analyze these factors. Accurate measurement is crucial for extracting meaningful insights and making informed decisions.

2.1 Traditional Methods

Historically, foot traffic analysis relied on manual methods such as on-site observers who recorded pedestrian movements. While this methodology can provide accurate data, it is labor-intensive, time-consuming, and limited in terms of scale. Furthermore, it may lead to observation bias, as human observation can be influenced by countless external factors.

2.2 Technological Advancements

Fortunately, advancements in technology have revolutionized foot traffic analysis, making it more efficient, scalable, and accurate. One of the primary technological tools used today is the footfall counter, which employs sensors, cameras, or Wi-Fi tracking to count the number of people passing through a specific area. These devices capture data continuously, ensuring a comprehensive and unbiased analysis of foot traffic patterns.

Furthermore, smart footfall counters can provide more in-depth insights by detecting additional metrics such as dwell time (the amount of time individuals spend in a specific area), entry and exit data, and even gender and age estimations. Leveraging this technology, businesses and city planners can gain a holistic understanding of foot traffic, enabling them to make data-driven decisions.

Understanding Demographic Data

Having explored the methods of measuring foot traffic, let us now focus on understanding the demographic data associated with foot traffic patterns. Demographic information encompasses various factors such as age, gender, income level, education, ethnicity, and family composition. Analyzing these data points helps paint a comprehensive picture of the pedestrian population within a given area.

3.1 Collecting and Analyzing Demographic Data

Demographic data can be collected through various sources, such as surveys, questionnaires, censuses, or by partnering with entities that already possess this information. Once collected, this data can be analyzed using statistical techniques to identify patterns, correlations, and trends among different demographic groups. These insights can provide businesses with a competitive advantage by guiding marketing and advertising campaigns, influencing product development, and enabling precise targeting of specific customer segments. For city planners, demographic analysis can inform urban development strategies, transportation planning, zoning decisions, and social service allocations.

Applications and Impacts of Foot Traffic and Demographic Analysis

In this final chapter, we explore the practical applications and far-reaching impacts of foot traffic and demographic analysis. The insights derived from these analyses have transformative potential for businesses, communities, and individuals alike.

4.1 Business Growth and Optimization

Foot traffic analysis helps retailers optimize store layouts, product placements, and marketing strategies. Understanding foot traffic patterns and demographics allows businesses to tailor their offerings to specific market segments, boosting customer satisfaction and loyalty. Furthermore, these analyses can identify opportunities for expanding physical store locations, targeting new markets, or adjusting business hours.

4.2 Urban Planning and Community Development

Demographic and foot traffic analysis contribute to informed urban planning decisions and community development initiatives. By understanding the composition of pedestrian populations, policymakers can plan infrastructure improvements, allocate public resources more efficiently, and enhance the overall livability of neighborhoods. Moreover, these insights can stimulate economic growth, attract investments, and promote equitable distribution of services and opportunities.

Looking Ahead: Future Trends in Foot Traffic Analysis

As technology continues to advance, the field of foot traffic analysis is bound to evolve alongside it. Future trends may include improved accuracy and resolution of footfall counters, integration of data from various sources for more comprehensive analyses, and the incorporation of machine learning and artificial intelligence to forecast foot traffic patterns.

Foot traffic and demographic analysis provide invaluable insights into the movement and characteristics of people in various settings. By leveraging a combination of advanced technology, accurate measurement methods, and demographic data analysis, businesses and communities can optimize their strategies, improve customer experiences, and maximize their overall potential for growth and development.

Legal and Permit Considerations in Placement

Vending machines have become an integral part of our daily lives, providing convenient access to a wide range of products. From snacks and beverages to personal hygiene items and electronics, these automated kiosks offer around-the-clock accessibility and instant gratification. However, before embarking on a venture to place vending machines in public spaces, it is crucial to understand the legal and permit considerations that accompany such placements. This chapter aims to provide a comprehensive overview of these considerations, guiding entrepreneurs and business owners towards successful and compliant vending machine placements.

Understanding the Legal Landscape:

To ensure the smooth operation of vending machines and protect the interests of all stakeholders involved, relevant laws, regulations, and permits should be thoroughly understood and adhered to. While legal frameworks may vary across jurisdictions, some common legal considerations in vending machine placement are as follows:

1. Zoning and Land Use Regulations:

Municipalities and local governments often dictate zoning and land use regulations that outline where vending machines can be placed. These regulations aim to maintain the character and integrity of specific areas and ensure public safety. It is essential to research and comply with these regulations before deciding on a vending machine placement location.

2. Business Licenses and Permits:

Obtaining the necessary licenses and permits is vital to operate a vending machine legally. Depending on the jurisdiction, a general business license may be required in addition to specific permits related to food handling, tobacco or alcohol sales, or any other products being dispensed through the vending machine. Failure to acquire the appropriate licenses and permits can result in fines, closures, or other legal consequences.

3. Health and Safety Regulations:

Health and safety regulations are of utmost importance when dealing with food or other consumable products. Vendors should ensure that their operations comply with local health codes, including proper food handling, storage, and sanitation practices. Regular inspections by health authorities may be required to maintain compliance.

4. Consumer Protection Laws:

Consumer protection laws govern business transactions to safeguard the rights and interests of customers. In the realm of vending machines, these laws often focus on accurate product labeling, pricing transparency, and fair business practices. Operators must ensure that the products in their machines meet all legal requirements and maintain clear and accurate pricing information.

Placement Considerations:

In addition to legal considerations, various practical factors must be evaluated when deciding the placement of vending machines. While the actual placement may often be at the discretion of the operator, it is crucial to assess some critical aspects before finalizing a location:

1. Foot Traffic and Target Market:

Understanding the target market and identifying high-foot-traffic areas is essential to maximize sales potential. Vending machines located in areas with high population density, such as shopping malls, airports, public transportation hubs, or office buildings, are more likely to generate substantial revenue. Analyzing customer behavior and preferences in a particular area can also help tailor product offerings to meet demand.

2. Competition Assessment:

Conducting a comprehensive analysis of existing competition is vital to identify market saturation and potential opportunities. Placing a vending machine in an area already saturated with similar offerings may yield suboptimal results. Instead, identifying underserved locations or specialized niches can provide a competitive advantage and increase profitability.

3. Accessibility and Space Requirements:

Ensuring accessibility for all users, including individuals with disabilities, is an ethical and legal responsibility. Vending machines should comply with accessibility guidelines, including the Americans with Disabilities Act (ADA) requirements, to guarantee that everyone can access and use the machines without discrimination. Additionally, evaluating the available space in potential locations is critical to determine if installation is logistically feasible and if there will be enough space for customers to comfortably utilize the machine.

4. Security and Maintenance Considerations:
Placing vending machines in secure areas can reduce the risk of theft, vandalism, or damage to the machines or products. Locations with appropriate surveillance systems, adequate lighting, and reduced risk of criminal activity should be prioritized. Additionally, regular maintenance and restocking schedules should be developed to ensure optimal functioning and customer satisfaction.

Understanding the legal and permit considerations in vending machine placement is paramount to establishing a successful and compliant operation. Pursuing a venture without careful consideration of legal frameworks can result in significant financial and legal penalties. Additionally, evaluating practical factors such as foot traffic, competition, accessibility, and security can contribute to maximizing profitability and customer satisfaction. In the subsequent chapters, we will delve deeper into specific legal considerations, uncovering challenges and providing guidance to navigate the intricacies of vending machine placement.

Chapter 4: Technological Edge: Embracing Innovation in Vending

In the ever-evolving landscape of commerce, vending machines have carved a permanent place. From providing snacks and beverages in office spaces to dispensing various products on busy street corners, vending machines have become an integral part of modern life. However, with the rapid advancements in technology, vending machines have also undergone a significant transformation. This chapter explores the technological edge that has revolutionized the vending industry and highlights the importance of embracing innovation to stay competitive in this ever-growing market.

Section 1: The Evolution of Vending Machines

Vending machines have come a long way since their inception in ancient Egypt, where they dispensed holy water. Over the years, these machines have witnessed numerous advancements, enabling them to be more efficient and versatile. From purely mechanical devices that relied on coins and levers to sophisticated automated systems, vending machines have kept pace with the changing demands of consumers.

The introduction of electricity in the late 19th century paved the way for significant improvements in vending machines. The first electric vending machines allowed for a wider range of products and increased convenience. With the advent of refrigeration technology, vending machines were able to dispense perishable items like sandwiches and sodas, marking a milestone in the industry.

Section 2: The Role of Technology in Modern Vending

The convergence of technology and vending machines has paved the way for unprecedented opportunities. Today, vending machines utilize cutting-edge software, hardware, and connectivity solutions to offer a seamless experience to consumers and operators alike. Let us explore the key technological advancements that have allowed vending machines to embrace innovation fully.

2.1 Cashless Payments: A Wave of Convenience

Gone are the days of digging through pockets for loose change to use in vending machines. The integration of cashless payment systems has revolutionized the way consumers interact with vending machines. With the rise of contactless payment methods such as mobile wallets and smart cards, vending machines have become more accessible and convenient for customers.

2.2 Data Analytics: Transforming the Vending Landscape

In the digital age, data is king. Vending machines equipped with IoT sensors and robust analytics systems can collect valuable data on customer preferences, purchasing patterns, and inventory levels. This data can empower operators to make informed decisions regarding product selection, pricing, and machine placement, ultimately enhancing profitability and customer satisfaction.

2.3 Digital Displays and Touchscreens: Enhancing User Experience

Transforming the traditional vending machine interface, digital displays and touchscreens have taken user experience to new heights. These interactive features offer detailed product information, customization options, and engaging visuals, attracting users and increasing sales.

2.4 Remote Monitoring and Inventory Management

With the advent of remote monitoring technology, vending machines can now be monitored and managed remotely. Real-time data on stock levels, machine performance, and maintenance requirements allow operators to optimize operations, reducing downtime and enhancing efficiency.

2.5 Machine-to-Machine Communication: The Future of Vending

As technology progresses, so does the capability of vending machines to communicate with each other. Through machine-to-machine communication, vending machines can share data, coordinate inventory levels, and strategize optimal pricing, creating an interconnected network that maximizes profitability for operators and convenience for consumers.

Section 3: Benefits and Challenges of Embracing Technological Innovations

3.1 Benefits of Technological Innovations in Vending

The incorporation of technological advancements in vending machines brings forth several benefits:

a) Increased efficiency and reduced costs: Automation and remote monitoring enable streamlined operations and minimize the need for manual intervention, thereby reducing costs and maximizing profits.

b) Customization and personalization: Digital displays and touchscreens allow vending machines to offer tailored experiences, catering to individual preferences and increasing customer engagement.

c) Improved inventory management: Real-time data analytics and machine-to-machine communication ensure optimal inventory levels, reducing wastage and ensuring availability of popular products.

d) Enhanced consumer experience: Cashless payments, interactive displays, and advanced features create a seamless and enjoyable experience for customers, fostering loyalty and repeat business.

3.2 Challenges in Implementing Technological Innovations

While technological innovations offer immense opportunities, they also come with their fair share of challenges:

a) Initial investment and costs: Integrating advanced technology into vending machines requires significant upfront investment, which may deter some vendors, particularly small-scale operators.

b) Technical complexity: The complexity of modern vending machines can present challenges in terms of maintenance, repair, and operator training. Keeping up with ever-changing technologies may also pose obstacles for some operators.

c) Cybersecurity concerns: The integration of cashless payment systems and data collection raises concerns about privacy and cybersecurity. Rigorous security measures must be implemented to safeguard customer information and prevent data breaches.

Section 4: Case studies: Success Stories in Technological Innovation

4.1 The Rise of Smart Vending Machines in Japan

Japan has long been at the forefront of technological innovations, and its vending machine industry is no exception. Smart vending machines equipped with facial recognition, machine learning, and IoT capabilities are now a common sight across the country. These machines can not only recommend personalized products based on historical purchase data but also adjust pricing based on demand, weather conditions, and other external factors.

4.2 Vendekin: Revolutionizing Vending in Emerging Markets

In India, Vendekin has emerged as a game-changer in the vending industry. By leveraging mobile apps, digital wallets, and IoT technology, Vendekin offers seamless cashless transactions, real-time inventory management, and remote machine monitoring. These innovative solutions have empowered small-scale vendors and bridged the gap between traditional retail and modern vending. Chapter 5 has explored the transformative power of technological advancements in the vending industry. From the evolution of simple coin-operated machines to the integration of AI-driven smart vending, technology has allowed these machines to become more than just convenient dispensers. By embracing innovation, operators can unlock countless opportunities to enhance efficiency, improve consumer experience, and stay ahead of the curve in a highly competitive market. The ever-evolving technological landscape promises an exciting future for vending, where convenience and innovation converge to reshape the way we access products on the go.

Cashless Transactions and Digital Payment Systems

In today's fast-paced and digitized world, the need for convenience and efficiency is higher than ever. From online shopping to contactless payments, consumers are increasingly relying on technology to simplify their lives. One area that has witnessed a significant transformation is the vending machine industry. Gone are the days when buyers needed exact change or had to struggle with jammed coin slots. In this chapter, we will explore the evolution of cashless transactions and digital payment systems for vending machines, their benefits and challenges, as well as the future prospects for this technology.

The Rise of Cashless Transactions

Cashless transactions have witnessed an exponential growth in recent times, transforming the way people make purchases. The increasing popularity of credit and debit cards, mobile wallets, and contactless payment methods have paved the way for cashless economies. Vending machine operators quickly realized the potential of incorporating such systems, keeping in mind the convenience they offer to consumers.

The Shift from Coins to Cards

Traditionally, vending machines required users to carry change in order to complete a transaction. However, this approach had its limitations. Users often struggled with insufficient change or the unavailability of coins, leading to missed sales opportunities. To overcome these challenges, vending machine manufacturers began introducing card payment acceptance systems.

Accepting credit or debit cards allowed users to make purchases even if they did not have cash on hand. This feature instantly gave vending machines an edge over traditional transaction methods. Moreover, it enabled consumers to track and manage their expenses with ease, using their preferred payment method.

Mobile Wallet Integration

With the advent of smartphones and the growing popularity of mobile payment apps, vending machines saw an opportunity to further enhance their capabilities. Mobile wallet integration into vending machines allowed users to make purchases by tapping their smartphones against the machine, reducing the need for cards altogether.

By leveraging Near Field Communication (NFC) technology, users can now complete transactions swiftly and securely. This contactless payment method provides the ultimate convenience, enabling users to leave their wallets behind and make purchases with just a few taps on their smartphones. Additionally, mobile wallets offer added security measures, such as biometric authentication, further safeguarding users' financial information.

Advantages of Cashless Transactions for Vending Machines

1. Convenience for Consumers: Cashless transactions eliminate the need for users to carry small change or search for ATMs. It provides consumers with the flexibility to make purchases at vending machines without worrying about the availability of cash.

2. Increased Sales Opportunities: By accepting card and mobile wallet payments, vending machines expand their potential customer base. Consumers who prefer digital payments are more likely to make purchases, resulting in increased revenues for vending machine operators.

3. Improved Inventory Management: Cashless transactions offer real-time data collection, allowing operators to monitor and analyze consumer preferences. By understanding which products are popular and which ones are not, vending machine operators can optimize their inventory, reducing waste and increasing profits.

4. Enhanced Security: Cashless transactions mitigate some of the risks associated with handling cash. For both users and operators, the digital payment systems provide secure and traceable

transactions, reducing the likelihood of theft or fraud.

5. Technological Advancements: Cashless transactions have evolved in line with advancements in technology, such as biometric authentication and two-factor authorization. These innovations further protect users' financial information and boost consumer confidence in using vending machines.

Challenges and Considerations

While cashless transactions for vending machines have numerous benefits, there are also challenges that need to be addressed.

1. Infrastructure and Implementation Costs: Upgrading vending machine systems to accept cashless payments can be an expensive undertaking. Operators must invest in new hardware, software, and security measures to ensure seamless integration.

2. Connectivity and Reliability: Cashless transactions require a stable internet connection to process payments effectively. Vending machines located in remote areas or regions with poor connectivity may encounter reliability issues, impacting the user experience.

3. Consumer Awareness and Adoption: Despite the rising popularity of digital payment methods, not all consumers are well-versed in using them. Promoting and educating users about the benefits of cashless transactions and their ease of use is crucial for widespread

adoption.

4. Maintenance and Technical Support: With the introduction of new payment systems, operators must also consider the technical support and maintenance requirements. Training staff to handle any potential glitches or failures is essential to ensuring a positive customer experience.

The Future of Cashless Transactions in Vending Machines

As technology continues to advance, the evolution of cashless transactions for vending machines is far from over. We can expect to see several noteworthy developments in the near future.

1. Artificial Intelligence (AI) Integration: AI can play a significant role in improving vending machine operations. From personalized product recommendations to dynamic pricing, AI algorithms can enhance the customer experience by providing tailored suggestions and promotions.

2. Biometric Authentication: With the growing emphasis on security and privacy, biometric authentication methods, such as fingerprint and facial recognition, may become standard features in cashless vending machines. These measures would ensure that only authorized users can initiate transactions.

3. Blockchain Technology: Blockchain, the decentralized and

transparent ledger system, has the potential to revolutionize the payments industry. By utilizing blockchain technology, vending machines could facilitate secure peer-to-peer transactions, eliminating the need for intermediaries and ensuring faster settlement times.

4. Integration with IoT (Internet of Things): Vending machines integrated with IoT devices can communicate and interact with consumers in real-time. For instance, IoT-enabled vending machines could notify operators when they're running low on specific products, optimizing inventory management and streamlining restocking processes.

Cashless transactions and digital payment systems have revolutionized the vending machine industry, offering users convenience, security, and greater purchase options. The shift from coins to cards and the integration of mobile wallets have made transactions faster and more secure. While there are considerations and challenges to overcome, the future prospects for cashless transactions in vending machines are promising. With ongoing technological advancements, we can expect to see further innovations that enhance user experiences and revolutionize the industry as a whole.

Remote Monitoring and Inventory Management Tools

In recent years, vending machines have become an integral part of our daily lives. From snacks and beverages to personal care items, these self-service kiosks offer convenience in various locations. However, managing and maintaining vending machines can be a challenging task, especially when dealing with multiple machines spread across different locations. That's where remote monitoring and inventory management tools come into play, revolutionizing the way we manage and operate vending machines. In this chapter, we will explore the benefits and functionality of these tools, how they enhance efficiency and profitability, and how businesses can make the most of this technology.

The Evolution of Vending Machine Management

Traditionally, managing and monitoring vending machines relied heavily on manual inspections and periodic inventory checks. This approach was not only time-consuming but also prone to human error, leading to inconsistencies in stock replenishment and revenue tracking. As technology advanced, businesses began exploring and implementing remote monitoring systems to streamline vending machine management.

Remote monitoring tools enable business owners and operators to remotely track the status of their vending machines in real-time. These tools gather and relay crucial information such as sales data, machine performance, and inventory levels, allowing operators to make data-driven decisions and respond promptly to machine maintenance issues or stock replenishment requirements.

Features and Functionality of Remote Monitoring Tools

1. Real-Time Sales and Performance Data

One of the key advantages of remote monitoring tools is the ability to obtain real-time sales and performance data from vending machines. This data provides valuable insights into consumer preferences and buying patterns, allowing businesses to optimize their product offerings. With accurate sales information readily available, owners and operators can identify top-selling items, adjust pricing strategies, and plan inventory management effectively.

2. Inventory Monitoring and Control

Inventory management is a critical aspect of running a successful vending machine business. Remote monitoring tools enable businesses to track inventory levels in real-time, alleviating the need for manual stock checks. Vending machines equipped with these tools can automatically generate alerts when certain products are running low or nearing expiration dates. This ensures efficient stock replenishment and reduces the risk of running out of popular items.

3. Remote Machine Diagnostics and Maintenance

In the past, operators had to physically visit each vending machine to diagnose and resolve technical issues. Remote monitoring tools have revolutionized this process by offering remote diagnostics and maintenance capabilities. Operators can now identify and troubleshoot machine malfunctions, such as coin jams or refrigeration problems, without leaving their desks. This significantly reduces downtime and improves the overall operational efficiency of vending machines.

4. Cash Management and Revenue Tracking

Effective cash management is essential for any vending machine business, and remote monitoring tools play a pivotal role in simplifying this process. These tools provide real-time cash and revenue tracking, eliminating the need for manual cash collection and reconciliation. Detailed reports on cash flow and sales revenue allow operators to monitor and analyze the financial performance of their vending machines accurately.

Benefits of Remote Monitoring and Inventory Management Tools

1. Enhanced Efficiency and Time-Saving

By automating various tasks such as inventory monitoring, sales tracking, and machine maintenance, remote monitoring tools streamline vending machine operations. Operators can focus on strategic decision-making and revenue generation rather than spending hours manually inspecting machines or reconciling cash. This automated approach saves time and enhances overall operational efficiency.

2. Improved Productivity and Profitability

Remote monitoring tools enable businesses to stay on top of their vending machine operations effortlessly. By leveraging real-time sales data, businesses can adjust their product offerings to meet consumer demands effectively. Optimizing inventory management reduces the chances of out-of-stock situations, ensuring maximum sales opportunities. Moreover, remote diagnostics and maintenance capabilities minimize downtime and maximize revenue generation.

3. Cost Reduction and Preventive Maintenance

Manual inventory management and machine maintenance can be costly endeavors, consuming valuable resources. Remote monitoring tools help in cost reduction by eliminating the need for unnecessary physical visits and offering preventive maintenance capabilities. Operators can proactively address maintenance issues, reducing repair costs and minimizing revenue loss due to machine failures.

4. Data-Driven Decision Making

With detailed sales reports and performance metrics at their fingertips, businesses can make informed decisions, driven by data insights. Remote monitoring tools not only enable businesses to identify consumer trends and preferences but also help in optimizing product placement, pricing strategies, and product mix. Data-driven decision making enhances profitability and ensures the success of vending machine businesses.

Remote monitoring and inventory management tools have revolutionized the vending machine industry. With their ability to provide real-time sales data, automate inventory management, and offer remote diagnostics, these tools offer numerous benefits for businesses, ranging from enhanced efficiency and profitability to reduced costs and improved decision-making. Embracing this technology allows vending machine operators to stay ahead of the competition, meet consumer demands, and deliver exceptional customer experiences. As the technology continues to evolve, we can expect even more advanced features and functionalities that will further transform the way we manage and operate vending machines.

Utilizing Data Analytics for Informed Decision-making

In today's fast-paced world, data plays a vital role in driving decision-making processes. From organizations to individuals, everyone is leveraging data analytics to gain valuable insights and make informed choices. Vending machines, typically seen as simple automated retail devices, are no exception to this trend. In this chapter, we will explore how data analytics can revolutionize the way vending machines operate, optimize inventory management, enhance customer experience, and ultimately, boost profitability.

The Rise of Data Analytics in Retail

Traditionally, vending machines were reliant on manual processes and limited insights to make business decisions. However, with advancements in technology and the availability of large volumes of data, vending machine operators now have access to a wealth of information that can transform their operations.

Data analytics empowers vending machine operators to make sense of data generated by various sources, including machine transactions, inventory records, and customer behavior. By aggregating, analyzing, and interpreting this data, operators can identify patterns, trends, and anomalies, enabling them to make data-driven decisions that optimize profits and enhance customer satisfaction.

Leveraging Machine Transaction Data

Vending machines generate vast amounts of transaction data every day - from individual purchases to overall sales and revenue. These data points present a goldmine of information that can be used to uncover valuable insights and drive decision-making.

For instance, analyzing transaction data can help operators understand the popularity of different products at specific locations and timings. By identifying high-demand items, operators can tailor their inventory, ensuring vending machines are stocked with customer favorites. In contrast, low-selling products can be replaced or removed to optimize inventory management and reduce waste.

Moreover, transaction data can provide valuable insights into pricing strategies. Analytics can help operators identify optimal price points that maximize sales while ensuring the products remain affordable and competitive. By analyzing correlations between pricing and sales volumes, operators can make informed decisions on pricing adjustments to drive revenue growth.

Understanding Inventory Management

Efficient inventory management is crucial for vending machine operators. Excessive stock levels tie up capital and increase the risk of spoilage, while inadequate stock leads to missed sales opportunities and dissatisfied customers. Data analytics can help strike the right balance by providing insights into inventory management.

By analyzing historical sales data, operators can identify seasonal demand patterns and adjust inventory levels accordingly. For example, during the summer, cold beverages might be in higher demand, necessitating increased stock levels. By using data analytics, operators can anticipate such trends and prevent stockouts during peak periods.

Additionally, data analytics can aid in identifying product performance gaps. By tracking sales data and comparing it with industry benchmarks, operators can identify underperforming products and take necessary actions. For instance, if a particular snack consistently falls below sales expectations, operators might consider replacing it with a more appealing alternative.

Enhancing Customer Experience

Customer experience is a key driver of success in any business, and vending machines are no exception. By leveraging data analytics, operators can gain valuable insights into customer behavior and preferences, leading to an enhanced experience for end-users.

One way to enhance customer experience is through personalization.

By analyzing purchase histories, operators can identify individual preferences and customize offerings. For example, a vending machine could recommend products based on previous purchases or offer targeted promotions to frequent customers. This level of personalization creates a more engaging and satisfying experience for customers, increasing the likelihood of repeat purchases.

Analyzing machine usage data can also help optimize the physical placement of vending machines. By identifying peak usage times and popular locations, operators can strategically position machines, ensuring maximum visibility and accessibility for customers. This data-driven approach can drive customer convenience and increase sales.

Predictive Analytics for Maintenance and Repairs

Maintaining vending machines in good working condition is crucial to avoid revenue loss and customer dissatisfaction. With data analytics, operators can implement predictive maintenance strategies, identifying potential issues before they become critical.

By analyzing historical machine performance data, operators can detect patterns that indicate an impending breakdown or component failure. This allows operators to schedule preventive maintenance at optimal times, minimizing downtime and reducing repair costs.

Furthermore, data analytics can help operators better understand machine usage patterns, enabling them to efficiently plan restocking and maintenance activities. By predicting when a machine is likely to run out of popular products or require maintenance based on historical trends, operators can proactively engage with suppliers and service technicians, ensuring uninterrupted service and customer satisfaction.

Data analytics has the potential to revolutionize the vending machine industry. By harnessing the power of data, operators can make informed decisions regarding inventory management, pricing strategies, customer experience enhancements, and maintenance planning. The actionable insights generated from data analytics enable operators to optimize vending machine operations, increase profitability, and remain competitive in a rapidly evolving market. As technology continues to advance, the role of data analytics will only become more vital, and vending machine operators who embrace this paradigm shift stand to reap significant benefits.

Maintenance Tech and Troubleshooting Solutions for vending machine

Vending machines are a convenient way for customers to purchase snacks, beverages, and other products on-the-go. As a maintenance technician responsible for these machines, your primary objective is to ensure that they are in optimal working condition at all times. Regular maintenance and prompt troubleshooting are essential in minimizing downtime and maximizing customer satisfaction. In this chapter, we will discuss various techniques, tips, and troubleshooting solutions to help you effectively maintain and repair vending machines.

Section 1: Preventive Maintenance

1.1 Cleaning and Sanitizing:

Regular cleaning not only keeps your vending machine looking presentable but also helps it function effectively. Wipe down all surfaces, including the display, product delivery area, coin slot, and keypad, using a non-abrasive, mild detergent. Pay special attention to any spillage, as it can lead to jammed or malfunctioning mechanisms. Additionally, sanitize the machine's interior by using a food-grade, non-toxic disinfectant to eliminate any bacteria or viruses.

1.2 Product Inventory Management:

Keeping a well-stocked vending machine is crucial in meeting customer demand and ensuring profitability. Create an inventory management system to track product expiration dates, restock levels, and popular items. Regularly check your inventory, removing any expired or spoiled products promptly. Additionally, analyze sales data to identify customer preferences and adjust the product selection accordingly.

1.3 Routine Inspection:

Performing routine inspections is essential to identify potential issues before they worsen. Start with a visual examination of the exterior, looking for any signs of physical damage, loose wires, or irregularities. Open the vending machine and check for loose or disconnected cables, worn-out components, or unusual sounds. These inspections should be conducted at least once a week.

Section 2: Troubleshooting Solutions

2.1 Power Related Issues:
If your vending machine is not powering on or experiencing intermittent power loss, there are several troubleshooting steps you can follow:

- Check the power outlet for any issues. Ensure it is well connected and supplying electricity.
- Inspect the power cable and check for damages or loose connections. If necessary, replace it with a new cable.
- Examine the power supply unit and verify that it is functioning correctly. Listen for any unusual sounds or signs of overheating.
- If all else fails, contact an electrician to inspect the electrical circuit and resolve any underlying issues.

2.2 Coin Mechanism Malfunctions:

Coins getting stuck or rejected are common problems with vending machines. Here are some troubleshooting steps you can take:
- Clean the coin slot by using compressed air to remove any debris or dirt.
- Check the coin chute for any blockages or foreign objects that may be obstructing the flow.
- Test the coin mechanism's sensitivity settings and adjust them accordingly to ensure proper recognition and acceptance of coins.
- If the issue persists, inspect the coin mechanism's internal components for any damages or signs of wear and tear that may require replacement.

2.3 Product Dispensing Problems:

If the vending machine fails to dispense products correctly, try these troubleshooting techniques:
- Ensure that the product shelves are properly aligned, allowing

products to move smoothly.

- Clear any obstructions or jammed products within the dispensing mechanism, ensuring it moves freely.

- Check the motor or coil responsible for dispensing and replace it if malfunctioning.

- Test the machine's sensors to ensure they are accurately detecting when a product is dispensed.

- Consider reprogramming the vending machine settings to adjust the dispensing portion size or reset the vend cycle.

2.4 Display or Keypad Malfunctions:

When the display or keypad on your vending machine is unresponsive or malfunctioning, follow these troubleshooting steps:

- Clean the display and keypad to remove any dirt or debris that might be obstructing proper operation.

- Check the wiring connections between the display/keypad and the machine's internal control board for any loose or damaged connections.

- Inspect the control board for any signs of burns or damages that might be affecting the keypad or display functionality.

- If necessary, replace the keypad or display module with new ones compatible with your vending machine model.

Maintaining vending machines requires a proactive approach to prevent issues and a systematic troubleshooting process to address problems promptly. By following the preventive maintenance tips provided in this chapter and applying troubleshooting techniques for common issues, you can ensure that your vending machines remain operational and provide a seamless experience for customers.

Chapter 5: Coins at Work: Maximizing Profits from Your Vending Venture

Welcome to Chapter 6 of our book, where we will delve into the world of vending machines and explore strategies to maximize profits from your vending venture. Vending machines have become a ubiquitous presence in our daily lives, providing easy access to snacks, beverages, and various other products. In this chapter, we will guide you through the ins and outs of operating a successful vending business, from choosing the right products to implementing effective marketing techniques. So, without further ado, let's dive in!

Understanding Vending Machines:

Vending machines are not mere dispensers of goods; they are mechanical entrepreneurs, working tirelessly to generate profits for their owners. However, to ensure success in this venture, it is vital to understand the different types of vending machines available, and select the most suitable one for your target market.

Snack vending machines are arguably the most common type, offering an array of crisps, chocolates, and other delicious treats. Beverage machines, on the other hand, cater to the thirst of customers by providing a wide selection of soft drinks, juices, and even coffee. Additionally, there are specialty vending machines, which offer more niche products like sandwiches, fresh fruits, or even personal hygiene items. Understanding your target market's preferences and needs will help you choose the right machines to maximize your profits.

Product Selection:

Choosing the right products to stock in your vending machines is crucial for attracting customers and maximizing your returns. Begin by conducting market research to identify popular items in your area and learn about customer preferences. Consider factors such as demographics, lifestyle trends, and dietary requirements when selecting your inventory.

Diversification is key in the vending business. Offering a variety of items, from healthy snacks to indulgent treats, allows you to cater to a wider customer base. Additionally, periodically refreshing your product selection keeps customers interested and encourages repeat sales. Remember, providing high-quality and popular products ensures that your vending machines remain profitable and in demand.

Pricing Strategies:

Setting the right price for your vending machine items can be a balancing act. Overpricing may deter customers, while underpricing could significantly impact your profits. Effective pricing requires thorough market research, understanding your costs, and analyzing your competition.

To determine your prices, consider multiple factors such as purchase cost, operational expenses, desired profit margins, and customer willingness to pay. Analyzing the prices set by your competitors can provide insights into the market standard and help you position your products competitively.

Aspects such as convenience, scarcity, and perceived value can also influence pricing. For example, vending machines placed in high-traffic areas with limited alternatives can command slightly higher prices. Always monitor your prices and be open to adjustments if necessary, keeping in mind that maintaining a balance between affordability and profitability is essential.

Placement and Location:
Location can make or break a vending business. It is crucial to strategically place your machines in high-traffic areas to maximize visibility and attract potential customers. Consider locations like office buildings, schools, hospitals, shopping centers, or gyms, where people tend to congregate and have a need for quick, on-the-go purchases.

Negotiating with property owners or managers for prime vending spots can be a game-changer. Offering them a percentage of your profits, rather than a fixed rental fee, can enhance the chances of securing valuable placements. Regularly assess the performance of your machines and, if necessary, relocate them to more profitable locations.

Maintenance and Service:

To consistently generate profits, your vending machines must be in optimal working condition. Regular maintenance and reliable service are essential to keep your customers satisfied and your machines running smoothly.

Create a maintenance schedule to ensure that your machines are cleaned, stocked, and serviced regularly. Perform routine inspections to identify and address any technical issues promptly. A well-maintained machine will encourage trust and reliability among customers, resulting in increased sales.

Marketing and Promotion:

Marketing plays a pivotal role in the success of any venture, and vending machines are no exception. Employing effective marketing techniques will help raise awareness about your machines, attract customers, and boost sales.

Utilize engaging visuals, such as attractive product displays and eye-catching signage, to draw attention to your machines. Utilize social media platforms and online advertisements to create buzz and promote your vending business. Consider offering limited-time promotions or partnering with local businesses to cross-promote each other.

Implementing Effective Marketing and Promotion Strategies

Vending machines have become an integral part of our daily lives, providing convenience and quick access to a wide range of products. From beverages and snacks to toiletries and electronics, these automated retail devices serve a variety of needs for consumers. However, with the increasing competition in the vending machine industry, it is crucial for operators to implement effective marketing and promotion strategies to stand out from their competitors. In this chapter, we will explore various techniques and tactics that can be employed to maximize the visibility, profitability, and customer satisfaction of vending machines.

Understanding the Target Market:

Before diving into marketing and promotion strategies, it is essential to understand the target market of your vending machine. Identifying your potential customers' needs, preferences, and behaviors will enable you to tailor your marketing efforts accordingly. Conducting market research, analyzing demographics, and surveying your current customer base will provide valuable insights into the target market's characteristics, allowing you to create targeted marketing campaigns.

Optimizing Vending Machine Locations:

The location of your vending machine plays a critical role in its success. Identifying high-traffic areas where your target market frequents is key to maximizing sales and visibility. Some prime locations for vending machines include office buildings, universities, hospitals, shopping malls, sports complexes, and transportation hubs. Collaborating with property managers, business owners, or event organizers to secure suitable locations can significantly increase your machine's accessibility, footfall, and profitability.

Eye-Catching Machine Design:

A vending machine's appearance can have a significant impact on attracting potential customers. Sleek, modern, and well-maintained machines are more likely to capture attention and generate interest. Consider investing in vending machines with appealing designs that align with the products being offered. Customizable wraps, vibrant graphics, and attention-grabbing signage can create visual appeal and make your machine stand out in crowded spaces.

Effective Product Display:

How your products are displayed can greatly influence customers' purchasing decisions. A clutter-free, well-organized interior with clear product categorization enhances the customer experience and encourages purchasing. Consider arranging popular or high-margin products at eye level for maximum visibility and accessibility. Additionally, make sure the products are well lit and regularly restocked to maintain an appealing and fully stocked display.

Innovative Product Selection:

The product selection of your vending machine should match the desires and preferences of your target market. While offering traditional snacks and beverages can be a safe choice, considering innovative and niche products can differentiate your machine from competitors. Incorporating healthy snacks, organic options, specialty drinks, ethnic foods, or even local artisans' products can attract a broader range of customers. Stay updated with market trends and consumer demands to ensure your product offering remains relevant and unique.

Pricing Strategies:

Pricing is a critical factor in attracting customers to your vending machine. It is essential to strike a balance between profitability and competitive pricing. Conduct a pricing analysis to determine a fair and reasonable price for each product, considering factors such as costs, market rates, and competitor pricing. Offering occasional promotions, discounts, or loyalty programs can also incentivize customers to choose your vending machine over others.

Harnessing the Power of Technology:

In the digital age, leveraging technology is crucial for effective marketing and promotion. Implementing cashless payment options, such as mobile payment apps or contactless cards, not only offers convenience to customers but also encourages impulse purchases. Consider incorporating interactive touchscreen displays on your vending machines to showcase product information, promotions, or even advertisements. Collecting data on customer preferences and purchasing patterns enables you to personalize promotions and improve customer satisfaction.

Engaging Social Media Presence:

Social media platforms have become powerful tools for marketing and promotion. Creating engaging and interactive content on platforms like Facebook, Instagram, and Twitter can help build brand awareness and foster customer loyalty. Share enticing images of your vending machine and products, run contests or giveaways, and encourage user-generated content by creating hashtags specific to your vending machine. Collaborate with popular influencers or local businesses to expand your reach and engage with a wider audience.

Partnerships and Collaborations:

Strategic partnerships and collaborations can significantly boost the visibility and profitability of your vending machine. Collaborating with complementary businesses, such as coffee shops, gyms, or office complexes, can lead to cross-promotion opportunities and shared customer bases. Consider forming alliances with suppliers or manufacturers to negotiate exclusive product offerings or discounts. Participating in local events or sponsorships can also increase brand exposure and attract potential customers to your vending machine.

Collecting Customer Feedback and Continuous Improvement:

Listening to customer feedback and continuously improving your vending machine's offerings and services is crucial for long-term success. Encourage customers to provide feedback through surveys, suggestion boxes, or social media platforms. Regularly review the feedback and identify areas for improvement, whether it be expanding the product range, addressing maintenance issues, or enhancing customer service. Demonstrating a commitment to customer satisfaction sends a positive message and increases the likelihood of repeat business.

Implementing effective marketing and promotion strategies for vending machines requires a thorough understanding of the target market, optimal machine placement, eye-catching design, effective product display, innovative product selection, competitive pricing, technological integration, engaging social media presence, strategic partnerships, and continuous improvement based on customer feedback. By employing these strategies, vending machine operators can enhance visibility, attract customers, increase sales, and stay ahead in this competitive industry.

Customer Engagement and Loyalty Programs

Vending machines have become a ubiquitous presence in our modern world. They offer a convenient and accessible way for customers to purchase a variety of snacks, drinks, and other items on the go. However, with the increasing competition in the marketplace, vending machine operators are faced with the challenge of ensuring customer engagement and loyalty to their machines. In this chapter, we will explore various customer engagement and loyalty programs that can be implemented for vending machines, aiming to encourage repeat purchases and build lasting relationships with customers.

Understanding Customer Engagement:

Before delving into the specifics of loyalty programs, it is crucial to understand the concept of customer engagement. Customer engagement refers to the emotional connection and level of active participation that customers have with a particular brand or product. In the context of vending machines, it encompasses how well customers interact with the vending machine and the overall experience they have during their purchase.

Components of Successful Customer Engagement:

Creating a successful customer engagement program requires a holistic understanding of the factors that contribute to a positive vending machine experience for customers. Let's explore some key components:

1. Vending Machine Placement and Aesthetics:

The physical placement of a vending machine plays a vital role in attracting customer attention and encouraging interaction. Placing machines in high-traffic areas such as shopping centers, office complexes, or college campuses increases the likelihood of engagement. Moreover, maintaining an aesthetically pleasing vending machine that is clean, well-lit, and visually appealing can significantly enhance customer experience.

2. Product Variety and Innovation:

Offering a wide range of products that cater to various customer preferences and dietary requirements is crucial for engagement. Regularly updating and introducing new products keeps customers intrigued and satisfied with the choices available. Innovative offerings, such as healthy snacks or organic beverages, can also provide a competitive edge and attract health-conscious customers.

3. User-friendly Interface and Interactive Features:

Customer engagement increases when a vending machine provides an intuitive and user-friendly interface. An engaging interface can include touchscreens, digital displays, video content, and interactive games or quizzes, creating a more dynamic and entertaining experience for customers during the purchasing process.

4. Cashless Payment Options:

Adopting cashless payment options, such as mobile wallets or contactless payment methods, can enhance customer convenience and encourage engagement. The ability to make quick and effortless payments eliminates the need for loose change, reduces transaction time, and simplifies the overall purchasing experience.

Implementing Customer Loyalty Programs:

Customer loyalty programs are an effective way to incentivize repeat purchases and foster a sense of loyalty towards a vending machine brand. Let's explore some strategies to implement a successful loyalty program:

1. Points-based Systems:

One common approach to loyalty programs is offering customers points based on their purchase value. These points can later be redeemed for discounted or free items. For example, customers earn one point for every dollar spent, and once they accumulate a certain number of points, they can exchange them for a free product or exclusive offers.

2. Tiered Rewards:

Implementing tiered reward systems can motivate customers to achieve higher levels of engagement. This approach involves dividing customers into tiers based on their purchase frequency or total spending. Each tier offers different rewards, with higher tiers providing more exclusive benefits, such as personalized offers, priority access to new products, or dedicated customer support.

3. Gamification and Challenges:

Adding gamified elements to loyalty programs can enhance engagement and provide a sense of achievement for customers. Challenges or competitions, such as "purchasing a specific product for a chance to win a prize" or "unlocking achievements for trying different products," can create excitement and encourage customers to explore the vending machine's offerings.

4. Personalized Offers and Recommendations:

Leveraging customer data and preferences can help create personalized offers and recommendations, which play a critical role in building loyalty. By analyzing purchase history or using customer input, vending machines can suggest relevant products or provide tailored promotions, showcasing that the brand understands and values individual preferences.

The Power of Data Analytics:

To drive customer engagement and loyalty effectively, vending machine operators must harness the power of data analytics. Data analytics enables valuable insights into customer behavior, preferences, and consumption patterns, enabling better decision-making regarding product offerings, placement, and promotions.

1. Tracking Customer Purchase Patterns:

By analyzing purchase patterns, operators can identify popular products, determine peak hours, and adjust the vending machine's inventory accordingly. This helps ensure that customers find their preferred items available, minimizing the chance of disappointment or missed opportunities for engagement.

2. Monitoring Customer Feedback:

Collecting and analyzing customer feedback is crucial for continuous improvement and maintaining customer satisfaction. Vending machine operators can implement feedback mechanisms, such as touchscreen surveys or QR code-based feedback submission, to gather valuable insights. Responding promptly to customer feedback demonstrates the commitment to enhancing their experience and strengthens loyalty.

3. Utilizing Social Media Platforms:

Social media platforms provide an excellent opportunity to engage with customers beyond the physical vending machine experience. Operators can create a social media presence, sharing updates, product announcements, and exclusive promotions to keep customers informed and engaged. Additionally, engaging with customers' comments, reviews, and questions on these platforms shows attentiveness and fosters a sense of community.

4. Integration with Mobile Apps:

Developing a mobile application dedicated to vending machine loyalty programs can further enhance engagement and customer convenience. Mobile apps can offer features like personalized recommendations, quick reordering of frequently purchased items, loyalty point tracking, and exclusive mobile-only promotions.

Upselling and Cross-Selling Techniques

The vending machine industry has undergone a significant evolution over the years. Gone are the days when vending machines were limited to selling just snacks and beverages. With advancements in technology and consumer demands, today's vending machines are equipped with a wide variety of products, catering to different needs and preferences.

While vending machines are an excellent means to automate sales and provide convenience, they can also serve as opportunities to increase revenue through upselling and cross-selling techniques. In this chapter, we will explore various strategies and tactics to maximize sales potential and enhance the customer experience within the realm of vending machines.

Understanding Upselling and Cross-Selling

Before diving into the techniques, it is vital to grasp the concepts of upselling and cross-selling. Upselling is the practice of encouraging customers to purchase a higher-priced version of the product they initially intended to buy. On the other hand, cross-selling refers to promoting complementary products or additions that complement the customer's purchase.

Upselling and cross-selling are effective techniques to increase the average transaction value and provide customers with a more comprehensive experience while using vending machines. By implementing these strategies, vending machine owners can add value to their offerings and boost profitability.

Creating an Appealing Vending Machine Display

First impressions matter, and a well-designed and attractive vending machine display can captivate customers and encourage them to explore the available options. To increase the chances of upselling and cross-selling, consider the following tips:

1. Clear Product Categories: Organize your products into distinct categories, making it easier for customers to navigate and find what they are looking for. Labels and signs indicating snacks, drinks, healthier options, or limited-time specials can grab attention and trigger impulsive purchases.

2. Eye-Catching Graphics: Utilize colorful and visually appealing graphics on your vending machine to captivate potential customers. Choose high-resolution images that evoke cravings or highlight the value-addition of upselling and cross-selling options.

3. Prominent Placement: Position upselling and cross-selling items at eye level within the vending machine, ensuring they are visually accessible and command attention. The top row or front panel are

typically the most visible spots within a vending machine, making them ideal for showcasing additional products.

Smart Product Placement for Upselling

Strategic product placement is essential to optimize upselling opportunities within a vending machine. Here are some effective techniques to consider:

1. Bundling: Offer bundled packages comprising a combination of popular snacks or drinks at a slightly discounted price compared to buying them separately. Emphasize the value and savings customers can enjoy by taking advantage of the bundle, encouraging them to purchase more items at once.

2. Size Upgrade: Present customers with an option to upgrade the size of their chosen drink or snack for a nominal price increase. For instance, a small coffee could be upsold to a medium or large size, attracting those who crave a little extra caffeine kick in the mornings.

3. Upselling Complementary Products: Analyze your vending machine inventory to identify products that naturally complement each other. For example, if your vending machine offers instant coffee, upsell it by placing single-serve creamers or sweeteners nearby. Highlight the convenience and enhanced taste that customers can experience by combining products.

4. Utilize Craving Triggers: Position products near complementary categories that can trigger cravings. For instance, place a selection of chips near the beverages section since they pair well with drinks and are desirable to customers seeking a savory snack.

Enhancing Cross-Selling Opportunities

Cross-selling techniques can significantly enhance the customer experience and create opportunities for additional sales. Consider incorporating the following strategies:

1. Dynamic Digital Menus: Utilize digital screens within your vending machines to showcase rotating cross-selling suggestions. These recommendations can change based on factors such as time of day, popular choices, or customer preferences, increasing the chances of enticing customers to explore complementary items.

2. Promotional Offers: Implement promotional offers that encourage cross-selling, such as a buy-one-get-one-free deal, a discounted price for purchasing a specific combination of products, or even a loyalty program offering incentives for cross-purchases.

3. Seasonal and Limited-Time Offerings: Introduce seasonal products or limited-time specials that customers can only find in your vending machine. This exclusivity creates a sense of urgency and curiosity, leading to increased cross-sales.

Training Vending Machine Operators

Vending machine operators play a crucial role in the success of upselling and cross-selling techniques. Educating and training operators to be proactive and knowledgeable about the products they offer can significantly impact sales. Consider the following:

1. Product Knowledge: Ensure vending machine operators are well-versed in the products available, including their features, benefits, and appropriate combinations. This knowledge equips them to make informed suggestions and tailor recommendations to individual customer preferences.

2. Salesmanship Skills: Provide training on basic sales techniques, such as active listening, building rapport, and making personalized product recommendations. These skills can enable operators to upsell and cross-sell effectively, as they engage with customers during the purchasing process.

3. Feedback and Monitoring: Regularly review sales data to identify patterns and trends. Use this information to provide actionable feedback to vending machine operators, helping them understand customer preferences and refine their upselling and cross-selling techniques accordingly.

Upselling and cross-selling techniques have the potential to revolutionize the vending machine industry by maximizing sales opportunities and delighting customers. By creating an appealing display, strategically placing products, and training vending machine operators, vending machine owners can create a win-win situation for themselves and their customers.

Embracing these techniques not only boosts revenue but also helps in continuously improving the vending experience and meeting evolving consumer demands.

Remember, upselling and cross-selling should be executed in a customer-centric manner, aiming to enhance satisfaction and go beyond just commercial gains.

By adopting these strategies, vending machine businesses can position themselves as reliable and convenient providers of a wide range of products, catering to diverse consumer needs.

Chapter 6: Growing Your Vending Empire: Scaling Up and Diversification

Congratulations on reaching Chapter 7 of this book, where we dive into the exciting world of scaling up and diversification within the vending industry. By this point, you have laid a solid foundation for your vending empire, and now it's time to take your business to new heights.

Scaling Up: Strategies for Expansion

Scaling up your vending empire requires careful planning and execution to ensure sustainable growth. In this section, we will explore a few key strategies that can help you expand your business to new locations and increase your profitability.

1. Location, Location, Location

As mentioned in previous chapters, the success of a vending machine heavily relies on its location. However, when scaling up, finding the right locations becomes even more crucial. Conduct thorough market research to identify high-traffic areas where your vending machines will attract the most customers.

Collaborate with local businesses, schools, hospitals, and office complexes to secure prime spots for your machines. Remember, the more strategic your locations, the higher the revenue potential.

2. Develop a Distribution Network

With a growing number of vending machines, it becomes more challenging to manually restock each one. Establishing a reliable distribution network is essential for maintaining regular inventory and reducing downtime.

Consider partnering with local suppliers, wholesalers, or even hiring a dedicated team to handle machine restocking and maintenance. Streamlining this process will allow you to focus on expanding your business instead of getting stuck in day-to-day operations.

3. Leverage Technology

In today's digital era, technology can play a significant role in expanding your vending empire. Invest in inventory management systems that allow you to track sales, monitor stock levels, and identify trends across multiple machines.

Additionally, explore cashless payment options such as mobile wallets or card readers to cater to customers' preferences and enhance convenience. Embracing technology will not only streamline operations but also create a more appealing vending experience for your customers.

Diversification: Exploring New Opportunities

While scaling up requires expanding within your existing niche, diversification allows you to explore new opportunities and broaden your vending empire. Let's delve into some effective diversification strategies that can help you maximize your profits and cater to different customer segments.

1. Healthy and Organic Options

As society becomes increasingly health-conscious, providing healthy and organic vending options can be a lucrative venture. Explore partnerships with local organic food suppliers and offer an array of nutritious snacks, drinks, and even freshly squeezed juices.

By capitalizing on the health and wellness trend, you not only cater to a growing customer base but also position your business as a provider of quality and conscious choices.

2. Specialized Vending Machines

Consider diversifying your vending empire by offering specialized machines that focus on specific products. For example, you could introduce machines exclusively for freshly brewed coffee, gourmet sandwiches, or even personal care items.

By tailoring your vending options to meet specific needs, you tap into niche markets and potentially attract a loyal customer base. Market research will help you identify areas where specialized vending machines can thrive and generate substantial profits.

3. Non-Food Vending

While food and beverages dominate the vending industry, don't overlook the potential of non-food items. Expanding your empire to include machines that sell personal care products, hygiene essentials, or even electronics can open up an entirely new revenue stream.

Identify customer needs in different environments, such as airports or gym facilities, and curate vending options accordingly. Providing convenience and essential items in unexpected locations will give you a competitive edge and fuel business growth.

Chapter 7 has provided you with insights into scaling up and diversifying your vending empire. Remember that successful expansion requires careful planning, strategic location selection, and embracing technology to streamline operations.

Diversification, on the other hand, allows you to maximize your profits by exploring different customer segments and capitalizing on emerging trends. Always tailor your offerings to meet market demands, focusing on health-conscious options, specialized machines, or venturing into non-food sales.

By incorporating these strategies, you will set yourself up for continued success and accelerated growth within the ever-evolving vending industry.

Reinvesting Profits for Expansion

In the ever-evolving world of business, the prime objective of any enterprise is to generate profits. For entrepreneurs, profits signify success and serve as a catalyst for growth and expansion. In the tantalizing realm of vending machines, reinvesting profits back into the business is vital to ensure continued success and to capture new opportunities in the market. In this chapter, we delve into the numerous possibilities and prudent strategies of reinvesting profits for the expansion of vending machines. Be prepared to embark on an exciting journey where financial acumen blends perfectly with the relentless pursuit of growth and increased market presence.

1. The Power of Profit Reinvestment:

In a business ecosystem where innovation and competition are rampant, reinvesting profits is the foundation upon which future growth is built. The potential to expand vending machine operations lies within one's ability to recognize opportunities and allocate resources systematically. By reinvesting profits, entrepreneurs inject much-needed capital into the business, enabling them to explore new avenues, enhance existing products, or even penetrate untapped markets. Profit reinvestment fuels expansion, and astute businesspersons understand that without such reinvestment, stagnation looms ominously.

2. Research and Development:

In today's fast-paced world, where consumer preferences and trends change swiftly, research and development (R&D) play a crucial role in vending machine expansion. Allocating a percentage of profits toward R&D ensures that businesses remain at the forefront of emerging technologies, product innovations, and vending machine versatility. By leveraging profits for R&D, vending machine operators can identify new product categories or even create products that cater to niche markets. Transformational discoveries and cutting-edge technologies made possible through R&D can pave the way for new revenue streams and unparalleled growth.

3. Geographic Expansion:

The physical presence of vending machines in strategic locations is paramount for their success. Profit reinvestment can be effectively utilized to expand geographic coverage. With vending platforms becoming increasingly sophisticated, operators can use profits to identify new markets with a high density of potential customers. By expanding into regions exhibiting untapped opportunities, businesses can increase sales and establish a dominant market position. Investing in efficient logistics and distribution channels using profits ensures a seamless expansion process.

4. Diversification of Offerings:

To satisfy evolving consumer demands, expanding the product portfolio of vending machines is imperative. Profit reinvestment can be used to explore new product categories or collaborate with complementary businesses to diversify the offerings. For instance, a vending machine that traditionally dispensed snacks and beverages could be expanded to include fresh food, organic snacks, or even specialty products. Through diversification, businesses not only attract a wider consumer base but also maximize the revenue potential of each machine.

5. Technological Advancement:

In the digital age, integrating cutting-edge technology into vending machines is a game-changer. By allocating profits toward the incorporation of smart features, such as cashless payment options, mobile applications, and telemetric systems, entrepreneurs can enhance the customer experience, streamline operations, and gain a competitive edge. Technological advancements can also improve inventory management, allowing businesses to reduce costs and minimize product wastage. Profit reinvestment in technology augments overall efficiency and prepares the groundwork for scalable growth.

6. Enhancing Customer Experience:

Creating a delightful customer experience is pivotal in the success of any business, and vending machines are no exception. By using profits to upgrade machine aesthetics, improve user interfaces, and enhance functionality, entrepreneurs can cultivate customer loyalty and encourage repeat business. Additionally, incorporating interactive displays, personalized recommendations, or even gamified experiences with rewards can captivate consumers and differentiate a vending machine from its competitors. The reinvestment of profits to enhance the customer experience leads to increased customer satisfaction, word-of-mouth referrals, and ultimately, heightened revenues.

7. Marketing and Advertising:

Profit reinvestment in marketing and advertising efforts is a powerful driver of vending machine expansion. By increasing the visibility of machines through targeted advertisements, social media campaigns, and strategic partnerships, businesses can attract more customers and generate higher footfall. Investing profits in market research can also aid in identifying untapped demographics or under-served locations that hold great potential for expansion.

Effective marketing strategies ensure that vending machines remain top-of-mind among the target audience, paving the way for further growth opportunities.

8. Strengthening Operational Infrastructure:

As the number of vending machines expands, it becomes crucial to strengthen the operational infrastructure. Utilizing profits to invest in back-end operations, logistics, and inventory management systems allows businesses to scale effortlessly and operate efficiently. Implementing centralized monitoring and error detection systems can enhance machine maintenance and minimize downtime, leading to increased customer satisfaction. By reinvesting profits into operational infrastructure, entrepreneurs create a solid foundation for further growth and expansion.

9. Training and Workforce Development:

Behind every successful vending machine operation is a skilled and motivated workforce. Reinvesting profits in employee training and development programs not only enhances productivity but also fosters a positive work culture. Training initiatives can focus on customer service skills, technical proficiency, or even entrepreneurial mindset development, empowering employees to contribute more to the success of the business. By investing in their workforce, businesses ensure that human capital becomes a catalyst for expansion.

10. Strategic Acquisitions and Partnerships:

Profit reinvestment can also be utilized for strategic acquisitions or partnerships that align with the long-term growth vision of the business. Acquiring smaller vending machine companies in lucrative markets or forming alliances with other industry players enables businesses to rapidly expand their footprint. Synergistic collaborations can lead to operational efficiencies, sharing of resources, and increased market reach, fostering the potential for exponential growth.

Reinvesting profits for the expansion of vending machines represents an opportunity for entrepreneurs to embrace change, stay ahead of competitors, and tap into new markets. This chapter explored a myriad of strategies that can be employed using the profits generated by these automated marvels. From reinvesting in research and development to geographic expansion, diversification, and incorporating cutting-edge technologies, the possibilities are endless. By ensuring that profits are intelligently deployed into strategic areas, businesses can propel their vending machine operations to unprecedented heights. So, buckle up and unleash the potential of profit reinvestment to embark on an exhilarating journey of growth and expansion in the vending machine business.

Managing Multiple Machines and Locations

In today's fast-paced and convenience-driven world, vending machines have become an integral part of our daily lives. From office buildings to shopping centers, schools to hospitals, vending machines cater to the needs and preferences of consumers across diverse locations. With the ever-increasing demand for on-the-go snacks and beverages, managing multiple vending machines and locations has become a challenging yet rewarding endeavor. In this chapter, we will explore the key aspects of effectively managing a network of vending machines, focusing on logistics, inventory management, maintenance, and customer satisfaction.

Logistics and Location Selection:

The success of a vending machine business largely depends on strategic location selection and efficient logistics management. Before installing vending machines, thorough research and analysis should be conducted to identify high-traffic areas with a target customer base. Locations such as transportation hubs, commercial districts, and educational institutions tend to offer a steady stream of potential customers. Additionally, considering factors like foot traffic, competition, and accessibility is crucial for success.

To streamline logistics, developing a comprehensive delivery and restocking schedule is imperative. Efficient routes should be designed to minimize travel time and fuel costs. Utilizing advanced logistics software can help optimize routing and scheduling, ensuring timely and accurate replenishment of products. Regularly reviewing and analyzing sales data can also aid in determining peak demand hours and adjusting restocking schedules accordingly.

Inventory Management:

An efficient inventory management system is critical to maintaining the profitability and customer satisfaction of vending machines. Keeping track of stock levels, monitoring sales patterns, and minimizing spoilage is paramount. Leveraging technology, such as vending management software, can simplify this process. These software solutions provide real-time data on inventory levels, sales trends, and popular products, allowing operators to make informed decisions.

To avoid stockouts and improve customer satisfaction, suppliers should be identified and contracts negotiated with them. Ensuring a reliable and responsive supplier ensures timely delivery of fresh products, reducing the chances of customer disappointment due to empty machines. Implementing a just-in-time (JIT) inventory management strategy allows operators to minimize excess inventory, reduce costs, and optimize the use of space within machines.

Maintenance and Machine Upkeep:

To run a successful vending machine business, regular maintenance and machine upkeep are vital. Routine inspections should be conducted to identify and address any technical issues or malfunctions promptly. Establishing a preventive maintenance schedule can help prevent costly breakdowns and minimize downtime.

Maintaining cleanliness and hygiene is of utmost importance. Regular cleaning of machines, including internal components and external surfaces, should be carried out to ensure product quality and enhance customer confidence. Training vending machine operators on proper maintenance procedures, including troubleshooting common issues, will empower them to address minor problems before they escalate.

Customer Satisfaction and Service Excellence:
Customer satisfaction is the driving force behind any successful business. Focusing on delivering exceptional customer service is crucial in the vending machine industry. First and foremost, ensuring that machines are stocked with popular and high-quality products caters to customer preferences. Conducting periodic surveys and analyzing customer feedback can provide valuable insights into consumer preferences and allow for adjustments to the product lineup.

To enhance convenience and engagement, offering diverse payment options, such as cashless payments and mobile wallets, should be considered. This enables consumers to make purchases quickly and conveniently, increasing the likelihood of repeat business. Regularly monitoring machine performance through data analytics can help identify trends, popular products, and areas for improvement, ultimately enhancing customer satisfaction.

Managing multiple vending machines and locations presents a myriad of challenges and opportunities for operators. By adopting effective logistics strategies, implementing robust inventory management systems, prioritizing maintenance, and providing exceptional customer service, operators can successfully navigate the complexities of this dynamic industry. Continual adaptation and improvement are crucial, as technology advances and consumer preferences evolve. With the right approach and dedication, managing multiple vending machines and locations can be a highly profitable and rewarding venture.

Introducing New Products and Varieties

Vending machines have become an essential part of our daily lives, providing convenient access to snacks, drinks, and various other products. Over the years, these machines have evolved from simple dispensers of a limited range of items to advanced, feature-rich devices with numerous customization options. In this chapter, we will dive into the world of introducing new products and varieties in vending machines, exploring the strategies and considerations involved in enhancing the consumer experience.

Understanding Consumer Behavior

Before we delve into the intricacies of launching new products and varieties in vending machines, it is crucial to understand consumer behavior. By gaining insight into what drives consumers' purchasing decisions, we can adapt our vending machine offerings accordingly.

One major aspect to consider is the changing dietary preferences and health consciousness among consumers. People are increasingly seeking healthier choices, driven by a desire for improved nutrition and a more balanced lifestyle. Therefore, incorporating health-conscious snacks, organic options, and low-sugar beverages into vending machine inventories can attract a wider consumer base.

Additionally, convenience plays a vital role in consumer behavior. The products available in vending machines should cater to individuals seeking quick and easily accessible solutions. Quick, on-the-go snack items, hot beverages, and microwaveable meals can attract busy individuals looking for immediate gratification.

Market Research and Product Development

Effective market research is crucial when it comes to introducing new products and varieties in vending machines. Identifying market trends, understanding consumer demand, and analyzing competitor offerings can provide invaluable insights for developing a winning strategy.

Before launching new products, it is essential to conduct taste tests and surveys to gauge consumer responses. This helps us ensure that the product meets quality standards and satisfies consumer expectations. Focus groups and online surveys can provide actionable feedback, helping refine the development process and optimizing product-market fit.

While researching new products, it is also important to consider the needs of specific demographics. Vending machines located in schools may require a different assortment of items compared to those in office buildings or gyms. Tailoring products to local preferences and consumer demographics increases the chances of success in specific markets.

Product Placement and Assortment

The location and arrangement of vending machines play a crucial role in their success. Once market research and product development are complete, it is important to determine the appropriate placement and assortment strategy.

Vending machines should be strategically placed in high-traffic areas with a large captive audience. Popular locations can include shopping malls, airports, train stations, offices, and hospitals. Collaborating with property owners or businesses in these locations can help secure prime spots for your machines.

To maximize sales, it is important to curate an assortment that appeals to customers. While variety is important, it is essential to strike a balance between offering a wide range of options and avoiding overwhelming consumers with too many choices. Placing popular and frequently purchased items towards eye-level will increase their visibility and encourage purchase.

Technology Integration

Integrating technology into vending machines can significantly enhance the consumer experience and increase overall sales. Modern technology allows for more advanced functionalities, such as touch screens, cashless payment methods, and interactive displays.

Cashless payment options, such as credit cards, mobile payment apps, or even biometric authentication, enable customers to make quick and convenient transactions. This not only caters to the growing number of people who prefer to go cashless but also allows for easier tracking of sales data and consumer preferences.

Touch screens and interactive displays can provide a user-friendly interface to showcase available products and their nutritional information. Providing detailed information about each item allows customers to make informed decisions and further reinforces the appeal of healthier options.

Digital advertising screens integrated into vending machines can also be used to promote new products and alert consumers to special deals or discounts. Engaging visuals and compelling content can catch the attention of potential buyers and drive sales.

Product Launch and Promotion

Once the research, development, and placement stages are complete, it is time to launch the new products and varieties in vending machines. However, a successful launch requires strategic planning and effective promotional campaigns.

Creating buzz around new product launches is essential. Utilizing various marketing channels, such as social media, email newsletters, and physical signage, can help generate excitement and attract attention.

Collaborating with popular influencers, bloggers, or celebrities who align with your target market can significantly boost product visibility and consumer interest. Offering them exclusive experiences with your vending machines or first access to the new items can create positive word-of-mouth and increase the chances of going viral.

Additionally, offering limited-time promotions or discounts on the new products encourages consumers to try them and increases their likelihood of making repeat purchases. Conducting sampling events, giving away free samples, or offering loyalty programs can further stimulate sales and build customer loyalty.

Continuous Improvement and Adaptation

Once the new products are introduced and well-received, the journey does not end there. Monitoring consumer feedback, analyzing sales data, and staying attuned to market trends are vital for ongoing success.

Continuous improvement should be an ongoing process. By actively listening to consumer feedback, vending machine operators can identify areas for refinement and adaptation. Regularly refreshing the product assortment based on consumer preferences, seasonal demands, and emerging trends keeps the vending machine offerings relevant and attractive.

Introducing new products and varieties in vending machines requires a comprehensive understanding of consumer behavior, effective market research, and sound product development strategies. By considering the evolving preferences of consumers, curating product assortments, leveraging technology, and implementing innovative promotional campaigns, vending machine operators can enhance the consumer experience, maximize sales, and stay ahead of the competition.